D0475961

Withdrawn from the Library of
The Queen's College, Oxford

This Septic Isle

COLL · REG · OXON

BIBL

This Septic Isle

Mike Barfield

EBURY
PRESS

1 3 5 7 9 10 8 6 4 2

Published in 2008 by Ebury Press, an imprint of Ebury Publishing
A Random House Group Company

Text and Illustrations © Mike Barfield 2008

Mike Barfield has asserted his right to be identified as the author of this
Work in accordance with the Copyright, Designs and Patents Act 1988

All rights reserved. No part of this publication may be reproduced,
stored in a retrieval system, or transmitted in any form or by any means,
electronic, mechanical, photocopying, recording or otherwise, without
the prior permission of the copyright owner

The Random House Group Limited Reg. No. 954009

Addresses for companies within the Random House Group
can be found at www.randomhouse.co.uk

A CIP catalogue record for this book is available from the British Library

The Random House Group Limited supports The Forest Stewardship
Council (FSC), the leading international forest certification organisation.
All our titles that are printed on Greenpeace approved FSC certified
paper carry the FSC logo. Our paper procurement policy
can be found at www.rbooks.co.uk/environment

Mixed Sources
Product group from well-managed
forests and other controlled sources
www.fsc.org Cert no. TT-COC-2139
© 1996 Forest Stewardship Council

Designed by seagulls.net

Printed in the UK by CPI Mackays, Chatham, ME5 8TD

ISBN 9780091925284

Withdrawn from the Library of
The Queen's College, Oxford

To buy books by your favourite authors and register for offers visit
www.rbooks.co.uk

To Jessica, the definition of wonderful.

Note: No aardvarks were harmed in the making of this book.

Foreword

Foreword

Robert Cawdrey's *A Table Alphabeticall* of 1604 is generally accepted to be the first proper English dictionary. It contains some 2,500 entries, though there are none beginning with the letters J, K, U, W, X or Y, thereby making it a second choice for most Scrabble fans.

Hidden amongst the two and a half thousand definitions are some delightful terms long since lost to us (snipperings, floscles, queach) and one joke. As far as I am aware, it is the first example in English of a humorous definition appearing in a dictionary. Your ribs are quite safe, however. For the word 'cymballe', Cawdrey supplies the comment 'an instrument of musicke, so-called'.

I like to think this was intended as a comic observation because there are no other jokes to be found elsewhere in the volume. Unless one includes Cawdrey's introduction, which claims the book will be of benefit to 'Ladies, Gentlewomen, or any other unskilfull persons'.

Of course, Dr Samuel Johnson is often erroneously credited with having compiled the first English dictionary, though his great work didn't appear until 1755. Less often is Johnson correctly identified as the godfather of its considerably more entertaining evil twin, the comic dictionary.

This is an oversight. Were it not for Johnson's comic definitions ('Oats – a grain that in England is generally given to horses, but in Scotland supports the people'; 'Lexicographer – a harmless drudge') few of us would – or indeed could – quote any of Johnson's dictionary nowadays.

From the point of view of a modern freelance humorist, there is also another, odder, aspect to Johnson's comic entries. Given how well-suited the dictionary form showed itself to joke-making – brevity being both the soul of wit *and* of definitions – it remains a surprise that Johnson's dictionary did not seemingly inspire comic imitations.

Instead there was a gap of some one hundred years during which time the comic lexicographical baton crossed the pond – from Doctor Sam to Uncle Sam. Or, more precisely, Uncle Am.

The work of the American columnist Ambrose Bierce remains the high water mark against which all humorous dictionaries will forever be judged.

This is thanks to *The Cynic's Word Book,* a dictionary-formatted collection of acerbic definitions penned by Bierce for various San Francisco journals over a twenty-five year period from the early 1880s onwards.

The book is better known today as *The Devil's Dictionary* – a title Bierce himself favoured but which is said to have been rejected at the time due to his publisher's religious sensibilities.

Not that Bierce cared much for religion. The book defines 'Pray' as 'to ask that the laws of the universe be annulled on behalf of a single petitioner confessedly unworthy' and a Christian as 'one who follows the teachings of Christ in so far as they are not inconsistent with a life of sin.'

Race, marriage, manners, fashion, business, warfare, the law – the whole of human life makes it into Bierce's book, and he regards it all with equal cynicism. Though perhaps his publisher *did* know best, after all. The book was published in 1906, the year of the San Francisco earthquake. Talk about divine retribution.

Bierce's dictionary inspired hundreds of imitators and spawned a vogue for daffy-nitions, deft-initions, and all manner of column-filling one-liners. Then came the radio comedians, followed by Hollywood, then television, and their insatiable appetites for comic material. This in turn generated a demand for gag books and saw the irresistible rise of compilations of humorous quotations, and comic dictionaries with, promised one blurb, '...wisecracks, gags, comic proverbs, arranged laffabetically from A to Z'.

The last quote comes from the cover of the *Comic Dictionary* compiled by the American Evan Esar, 'the noted authority on humor'. He died at the age of 96, having already heard and recorded so many jokes that he now rarely laughed other than out of politeness.

Poor man. One feels genuinely sorry for him.

Few comic dictionaries get written these days. The British newspaper humorist 'Beachcomber' produced a great one for his collection, 'Morton's Folly' – but that was back in 1933. If I can make any claim for the book you have before you now, it is that I wrote all of it myself. Good of you to take the blame, some will say. Four centuries on, it has about as many entries as Robert Cawdrey's *Table Alphabeticall*. At the risk of sticking my neck out, I'd also contend it has easily twice as many jokes. It also shares an ambition common to all English dictionaries, comic or otherwise, from Cawdrey's era onwards: to reflect its time.

Glancing through *This Septic Isle*, some may feel that my particular mirror has a tendency to distort, and even that it has one or two nasty cracks in places, but I'm confident we can all still recognise ourselves in it.

And remember, ultimately, that I'm hoping to make you laugh. Those people who invent terms like 'asymmetrical warfare', 'friendly fire', 'companion animal', 'life partner', 'parallel parenting', 'collateral damage', 'differently abled', 'downsizing', 'gender realignment', 'attention deficit', 'quality time', 'thinking outside the box' – *they're* being serious.

Mike Barfield, 7th April 2008

a

'aardvark

Aardvark | South African burrowing mammal. Harmless, never hurt anyone.

Abandon, gay | Same as straight abandon, but with a lot more shrieking and hand flapping.

Abbreviation | Long word with, ironically, no obvious shorter alternative.

Ability | A modern handicap to promotion.

Able-bodied | Any person refused Invalidity Benefit is deemed to be able-bodied.

Absent-minded |

Absinthe drinker, the | Iconic French painting of a miserable person in a pub. A forerunner of the modern British TV soap.

Absolution | Religious slate-wiping. Not to be confused with AbsSolution – the trendy new gym for men!

Abuse | The motorist's greeting to his fellows.

Accident | 1. A pregnancy. 2. Any negligent or malicious behaviour performed by someone with a clever lawyer. 3. Any negligent or malicious behaviour by a member of the Establishment.

Accident prone | To fall on your front, as opposed to falling on your back ('accident supine').

Acclaimed | Marketing terminology for any book or film that fails to win awards.

Accommodating | Putting up with Lynne Truss's pickiness over grammar.

Accomplish | A very drunk criminal's partner in crime.

Accurate | Adjective used to describe a newspaper article with more than half of its facts correct.

Acid rain | Precipitate precipitation. The major British export to Scandinavia.

Acrimonious | Word only ever attached to divorce cases. A solicitor's synonym for expensive.

Acquaintance, casual | A friend who never dresses up.

Acronym | The new language of Europe.

Action-packed | Film review term meaning: 1. Noisy. 2. Nearly plot-free.

acrobat

Acupuncture | The ancient Chinese practice of owning a real Christmas tree.

Additives, food | The sole cause of bad behaviour in children whose parents have no time to cook for or look after properly.

Admirer, secret | See Stalker.

Ad nauseum | Sick of adverts.

Adolescence | Awkward period between local authority care and prison.

Advent | Popularly supposed to be a corruption of 'advert'.

A dog is for life, not just for Christmas | Message not heeded in South Korean restaurants.

Adult | Anything too dull, ridiculous or disgusting to show to children is said to be adult.

Adultery | A place where kids can leave adults while they go on holiday.

Advance, technological | Money for writing dull book about gadgets.

Adventure playground | An ironic use of the word 'adventure' in the context of some old tyres and a pit containing bark chippings.

aerial

aerial view

Aerobatics | See Heathrow, near miss.

Affordable housing | See 1. Shoebox. 2. Tent.

Afterburn | See below.

Aftershave | See above.

Aga | A writing tool.

Agamemnon | An ancient Mycenaean stove.

Ageless | Dead.

Agitator | A nervous potato.

Agnus dei | Like Doris Dei, but more sinister.

Agony column | The *Daily Mail* leader.

Agrochemical | 1. Alcohol. 2. Testosterone.

Airbrush | A cockney hairbrush.

Airhead | See Sex doll.

Aladdin's cave | Iraqi criminal's hiding place still to be unearthed by US forces.

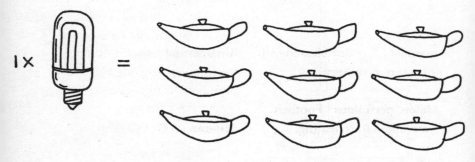

Aladdin: the update

alien

illegal alien

Alarmist | A realist blessed with the gift of prophecy.

Albion, perfidious | Football team noted for cheating.

Alderman | Superhero with the amazing ability to turn into a riverside tree.

Alien, illegal | Alien with no professional skills such as plumbing or medicine.

Also-ran | A British athlete.

Altar ego | A show-off vicar.

17

alphabetti spaghetti,
Saudi Arabia

Amalgamation | A gathering of dentists.

Amateur | A person too stupid to profit from the talent they possess.

Angel | Tabloid newspaper term for any nurse not on a picket line.

Apology | The smallest size of type used in a newspaper.

Arbitrary | Loser's assessment of any ruling made against them by a High Court judge.

Army | Collective noun for British sports fans overseas.

american

afro-american

animal magnetism

Aroma | Advertisers' term for the faint smell possessed by instant coffee.

Art, modern | Any painting or sculpture executed according to principles developed over 100 years ago.

Arthritis | Chronic condition soon to be the subject of a Joint Working Party.

Assembly | Frustrating period for all home-build furniture purchasers.

Assets | A model's breasts.

Assistant, shop | A paid observer.

Astrology | Archaic pseudo-science in which people who don't understand how a microwave oven works seriously believe that distant lumps of rock control their lives.

Atheist | Person who worships Richard Dawkins.

Avocado | A lavatory-coloured fruit.

baardvark

B | An obsolete A level exam grade.

Baardvark | South African anteater with a gift for poetry.

Babyhood | The smallest size of hoodie available.

Baby monitor | The modern child's introduction to surveillance society.

Babysitter | Any 14 year-old-girl paid to look after children not her own.

baby bouncer

Baccalaureate | Tobacco industry poet in residence.

Bachelor, confirmed | Any as-yet-unconfirmed heterosexual male.

Bachelor of arts | Stephen Fry, Sir Ian McKellen, Gilbert, George, etc.

Backbencher | Any obscure MP with a handy view of the gap between their leader's shoulder blades should their party start to slip in the polls.

Backdoor | Term beloved of anti-immigrationists: the Polish tradesman's entrance.

Backgammon | Bacon owed in arrears.

Backhand | A stroke in tennis.

Backhander | A stroke of luck.

Backlash | Three letters to *The Times* complaining about something.

Back out | Commonest cause of workplace absence.

Backpack | An ergonomically designed high-performance rucksack, now best avoided by the olive-skinned and bearded.

Backroom boy | 1. A boffin. 2. A kidnap victim.

Backyard, not in my | Principle exercised over housing developments, but equally valid for barbecues, decking, and squirrels.

Bad hair day | A national holiday in many of the former Soviet Bloc countries.

monkday

chewsday

windsday

furzeday

flyday

flatterday

shunday

bad hair days

Badly off | Without digital television.

Badmouth | Result of no longer being able to afford dental treatment.

Bag, brown paper | Recyclable, environmentally-responsible wrapper for pornography

Bagatelle | A French bag lady.

Bag lady | Anya Hindmarch, Lulu Guiness, etc.

Bail | The small charge that criminals must pay to the court in order to get to re-offend prior to trial.

Bail, to jump | A cricketing victory celebration.

Bairn | 1. *Scots*. A child. 2.*Scouse*. A wound caused by heat.

Baked Alaska | Likely consequence of climate change.

Balderdash | 1. Rubbish 2. What hairless men think they possess. (See 1.)

Ballot box | Zimbabwean wastepaper basket.

Ban, blanket | Dastardly EU proposal to spread the use of duvets.

Bandit | What the government did to public smoking.

Banger, old | Sausage past use-by date.

Bhangra | An Indian sausage.

Banish | The language of Bain.

Bank holiday | A national automobile rally.

Bank note | A multi-denominational cocaine delivery unit.

goner kebab

beef burner

ash browns

conflagration chicken

TO DRINK:

coke

cup of char

coala

barbecued foods

Bankrupt | Any company which runs out of other people's money is declared bankrupt.

Bar, called to the | 1. A barrister. 2. Anyone whose car is blocking the pub car park.

Barbecue | Device for ruining meat outdoors.

Barber's pole | Quite likely, nowadays, given t'skills gap.

Barefaced lies | Extravagant shaving crème claims.

Bargain | Any unwanted item bought solely because it was reduced in price. A good clue to these items' real value is that they are often found in a bargain bin.

Bargepole | Device with which most sun-hungry Britons would refuse to touch an inland waterways holiday.

Barium meal | No worse than most other hospital food.

Barnacle | A Mormon farm building.

Barrage | The standard unit of complaint.

Barrister | Highly paid wig-wearer. See also John, Elton.

Basic English | Wt, fanx 2 txtng, mst kds aint evn gt.

Basic model | What the luxury version of a car reverts to after having its stereo stolen.

Bash Street | The only British school still to retain traditional teaching methods and small class sizes.

Basket case | Driven mad by modern shopping. See also 'Off your trolley'.

Bastard | Any person who causes one some mild irritation

Batsman | The acceptable face of hit-and-run.

BBQ | A commonly used abbreviation. It stands for Burnt Black Quickly.

Beanbag | Dr Gillian McKeith.

Beanpole | East European catwalk model.

Bear Garden | Euphemism for a noisy, raucous place. Easily confused with beer garden.

Beard | Likely facial appendage of oddly dressed, quasi-religious figure with suspicious luggage and many hours of flying experience, e.g. Father Christmas.

Bearing, military | Vital component missing from British battlefield tanks.

Beat | That area of pavement that flashes past the window of a police panda car.

Beatitude | Mild, compared to waspatitude.

Beaujolais nouveau | Wine so reliably foul that the world rushes to get it all drunk and out of the way as quickly as possible.

Beauty | Now in the nipped, lifted, and lasered eye of the beholder.

Beauty spot | A wood with a car park attached.

Beaver away | To work hard on removing one's pubic hair.

Bed and breakfast | The modern short-term relationship.

Bed-blocking | The frustrating failure of the old to die on demand.

Bedpan | About the only pan some TV chef has yet to endorse.

Bedroom | A chamber of congress.

Bedside manner | The skill with which a GP is able to disguise their lack of sincerity.

Bee | A non-unionised food-industry worker.

Beeline | The confidential telephone counselling service for distressed hive workers.

Before and after | Two adjacent photographs of the same person used to demonstrate the amazing results achievable after a simple course of airbrushing.

Beforehand | Tennis stroke favoured by those with psychic powers.

Beggars belief | That a dog on a bit of string is a copper-bottomed sales boost.

Being, supreme | Diana Ross.

Bellow | Standard level of human voice seemingly required to conduct any phone conversation on public transport.

Belly flop | Ineffectual dieting.

Belly laugh | Hilarity provoked by the sight of British tummies on the beach.

Belt and braces | Compulsory requirements for any car-driving teenager.

Benchmark | 'Jodi 4 Daryl', 'Yur mum's a slag', 'F*CK U', '4 seX call Sami', etc.

Beneath my dignity | Euphemism for 'Not well enough paid'.

Bespoke tailor | Tailor with a bicycle.

Best before date | September 11th 2001.

Best practice | An elaborate, expensive and time-consuming business process to ensure good results. So-called because it is 'best-practised' by others.

Bestseller | 1. Book with a title faintly familiar to high court judges. 2. Any book with a startling theory about Jesus' bloodline – including, of course, the Bible.

Bete noire | A despised adversary – not necessarily French.

Better half | For most of us, our upper half.

Betwixt | In possession of a Twix.

Beverage | Word only ever encountered on menus. See also 'gratuity', 'pan-fried', 'jus', 'patron', etc.

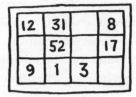

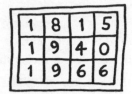

bingo

jingo

Bias | 1. Any prejudiced account which fails to tally with one's own prejudices is said to show clear bias. 2. A childhood prefix as in 'Bias sweets', 'Bias ice cream','Bias trainers', etc.

Bible, the | Any fully-comprehensive guide-book such as a car-maintenance manual etc.

Bifocals | Spectacles incorporating corrective lenses for both near and distant vision thereby affording the owner the convenience of mislaying two pairs of glasses at once.

Bigamy | To marry in haste and repeat at leisure.

Big Bang | That split-second cosmic catastrophe which set in motion a train of events that so far has produced the universe, the planets, all known and unknown forms of life, and individual sachets of microwaveable sugar-free frozen porridge, among other things. No wonder the concept is beyond the comprehension of most people.

Bike lane | Jeremy Clarkson's route of all evil.

Bikini line | The queue outside any rock star's trailer.

Bilingual | The ability to enjoy a subtitled film without one's TV dinner going cold.

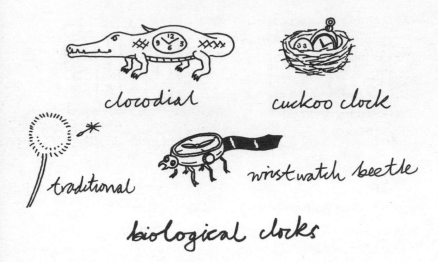

clocodial

cuckoo clock

traditional

wristwatch beetle

biological clocks

Bill, the | Called for at the end of a meal, especially when the diner cannot pay.

Billionaire | Any Russian formerly high up in the Communist Party.

Bill of health, clean | Anything in good working order is said to have this. Ironically, it is rarely applicable to the NHS.

Bin end | The termination of weekly collections.

Bin Laden | Result of fortnightly collections.

Binge drinking | Drinking *like* a doctor, instead of as *advised* by a doctor.

Bingo | Pastime of chiefly older women who sit waiting for their numbers to come up.

Biodegradable | Term interpreted to mean 'litter-able'.

Biological clock | Like the sundial and the longcase

clock, another timepiece set to be rendered redundant by advances in science.

Birds of a feather… | Get incinerated together. (Old DEFRA proverb.)

Birdbrain | Bill Oddie.

Birth | A surgical procedure.

Birthday suit | Legal term. A paternity claim.

Bisexual | Sleeps happily with both men and women, but isn't a cat.

Bit part | Oral sex hazard.

Bite the hand that feeds you | Ever-present burger bar risk.

Bitter end | The all-conquering onward march of lager.

Black | The only colour trendy fashion-designers wear despite insisting that everyone else should be in purple, green, etc.

Black death | See Gun crime.

Blame culture | What right-wing commentators love to do.

bi-polar explorer

Blind, in the kingdom of the |
...The one-eyed man is Gordon
Brown.

Blind with science | See 'Laser,
careless use of'.

Bling | Noise made by
Chinese telephone.

Blinking nuisance |
Any LED-encumbered
modern device.

Blitz spirit | Drink
popular with nostalgic tramps.

Blondes | 1. According to
social anthropologists, a dying
breed. 2. A dyeing breed.

Blood test | Routine anti-
doping procedure from which
many athletes run a mile.

Bloody Sunday | Post 'The
Troubles', any Sunday spent
doing DIY or using power tools.

Blouse, big girl's | Blouse
needed by increasing number
of overweight small girls.

Blow-up doll | An attractive
suicide bomber.

Blow your own trumpet |
Sound advice in the event of
bird flu.

Blow-by-blow account | George Michael's secret diaries.

BLT | A Bacon, Lettuce and
Tomato sandwich. Fortunately
this acronymic system doesn't
extend to Smoked Ham,
Iceberg and Tomato, or indeed
Chicken, Rocket, Avocado and
Pesto.

Blue moon | Lunar event
of great excitement to
astronomers and long-married
couples alike.

Bodger | An inept badger.

Bodily fluids | Lager, cola,
hooch, mcShake.

Body bag | An ill-fitting military uniform.

Body language | Arsehole, c*nt, prick, etc.

Bogeyman | An unhygienic golfer.

Bollard | A cross between a bore and a dullard. Best not run into.

Bomber, suicide | Person determined not to die alone.

Bone china | Take enough Viagra and you probably could.

Book end | Harry survives. Marries Ginny. Their kids go to Hogwarts.

Book-keeper | A former good friend about whom one would think twice before lending them anything in future.

Boomerang | Eco-friendly toy: impossible to throw away.

Boomeringue | Aboriginal confectionery.

Bore, crashing | A repeatedly failing computer.

Boring | Anything young people either fail to appreciate or cannot understand.

Born again | Result of rewinding maternity home video back past baby's first appearance.

Bothersome | What wasps do in August.

Bottlebank | A large metal receptacle for waste glass. Called a bank because of the ease with which one can make a deposit and the difficulties encountered in attempting a withdrawal.

Bottom line | See VPL.

Boundless enthusiasm | Over-enthusiasm.

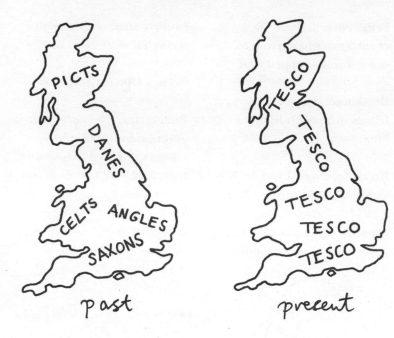

Britain : Past & Present

Bowdlerised | Flipping ruined.

Boxfresh | Only recently interred.

Boyfriend, on-off | See Rabbit, rampant.

Brand name | Thanks to product placement, now one of the biggest names you'll see in a Hollywood film.

Bravado | The courage needed to go bra-less.

Brazen | A shameless dried grape.

Brazilian | Beauty treatment for those with a Latin streak.

Bread, sliced | The worst thing since unsliced bread.

Break cover | Usual occurrence when trying to open shrink-wrapped CDs.

Breakdown, nervous | Any car failure in a poorly lit inner city area.

Breast-feeding | Every baby's right (and left).

Brewery | The standard unit of government incompetence.

Brought to book | Result of seeing movie version first.

Brine | Upper-class brown.

Budget, the | An annual government economic statement of such importance that children's television has to be disrupted by its broadcast.

Buffer zone | Trendy website for elderly gentlemen.

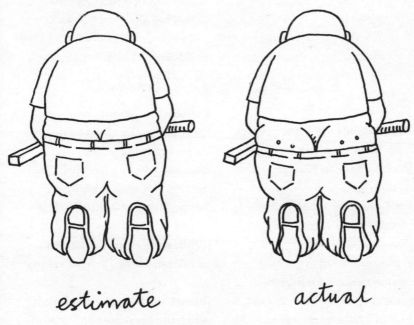

estimate   actual

builders' bums

Bungs

championship

premiership

Buffet | The adult version of pick 'n' mix.

Buggy, baby | The satanic offspring of the union between a deckchair and a shopping trolley.

Builder, Bob the | About the only British builder getting work in Eastern Europe.

Built-in obsolescence | See Middle age.

Bulbs, energy-saving | Eco-friendly illumination. If only the glow they produced was half as bright as the idea behind them.

Bull bar | Grille sported by 4X4s to avoid road casualties damaging their paintwork.

Bulldozer | The town planner's off-road vehicle.

Bullshit | A manure of speaking.

Bumbag | See Colostomy.

Bung | Footballing term. The largest amount of money that will fit comfortably inside an envelope.

Bungalow | Dwelling with only one habitable story, e.g. a two-storey house on a flood plain.

Burn-out | See Portable barbecue.

Button mushroom | Edible fungus rapidly being replaced by its Velcro equivalent.

Buxom | What a bronco does to inexperienced cowboys.

Buzzword | Any word on which a *Just a Minute* panellist slips up.

Bypass | Road that spares motorists the chore of driving through some picturesque town or village.

busman's holiday

C

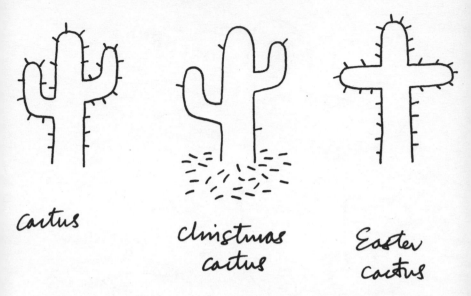

cactus

Christmas cactus

Easter cactus

C | Vitamin found in chemists' and, it is rumoured, certain fruits and vegetables

Cab, taxi | A mobile debating chamber.

Cabinet government | System of political decision-making in which all attending are entitled to an opinion – the opinion in question being that of the Prime Minister.

Cabriolet | Soft-topped car. From the French for 'easily broken in to'.

Caffeine | Drug known to trigger increased heart rate – especially when you realise it's over two quid a cup.

Cagoule | Garment very nearly as ugly as its name.

Calculus | Branch of mathematics in which letters replace numbers when deducing rates of change – though nowadays increasingly fewer x-pupils know y.

Calendar, nude charity | A now-hackneyed assault on good

WOOOOHHH!

caghoul

taste for which the punishment should match the crime – 12 months.

Call box, public | An advertising hoarding for prostitutes.

Call, cheap rate | Description of any call made on someone else's telephone.

Call me Ishmael | Archaic novel opening now updated to 'Txt me, Ishml'.

Call of the wild | The need to defecate outdoors.

Call-out charge | Money paid to plumber for privilege of offering him work.

Camel | Saharan off-road vehicle.

Cameo | Any brief appearance by some highly paid famous actor in a bad film that is long enough to warrant a fee but too short to attract any blame.

Camera-ready | What Boris Johnson so rarely seems to be.

Camera-shy | Nervous about exceeding 29 mph.

Cameron Highlander | Rare Tory-supporting Scotsman.

Camouflage trousers | Popular military-style legwear with distinctive broken pattern. Ironically, this makes them the most readily located items in the trouser section.

Campaign, military | A series of recruitment ads for the armed forces.

Campaign trail | The Lib Dems' road to nowhere.

Can of worms, whole new | Handy standby for early birds who just can't be arsed.

Canape | The plaint of the penniless Scotsman.

Canard | What Vinnie Jones reckons he can-is.

Cancer | A wasting disease. First the patient wastes time before seeing their doctor. Then the hospital wastes time before seeing the patient. Then the patient wastes their breath asking for expensive treatments.

Can

Can-Can

Santa   Victorian chimney boy   Satan   Sooty   Sweep

carbon footprints: a selection

Cannabis | So-called 'gateway drug'. Not to be confused with tobacco – now a doorway drug.

Cantaloupe | A circular horse-racing track.

Capable, highly | Official description of any minister not up to his job.

Cap in hand | Waiting for emergency dental work.

Capon | One of the two main superhero clothing options.

Captivate | An octet of hostages.

Caravan | A car-drawn home, always given pride of place at the front of any long, slow-moving procession of vehicles.

Carbohydrates | Important food group, giving the body the energy to go and get more biscuits.

Carbonation | Process that renders liquids drinkable to the young.

Carbon footprint | Mark left on carpet by Santa.

Carbuncle | Close male relative on the Atkins diet.

Carcinogenic | Property of anything drunk, eaten, or inhaled that is pleasurable.

Cardiology | The study of knitwear.

Carefree | 1. Drunk. 2. Sleeping around.

Care home | Oxymoronic residence for the old or infirm.

Carnal knowledge | Now a Key Stage 3 requisite.

Carnivorous | Morally outrageous dietary trait forgivable only in the pets of vegetarians.

Carrot and stick | A superwaif and her lunch – or, rather, vice versa.

Car wash, automatic | Labour-saving device sparing the car owner the many hours that would otherwise be spent gouging their paintwork by hand.

Cash | Outmoded currency kept alive solely for the convenience of builders.

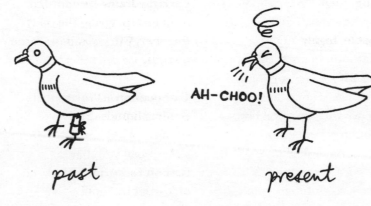

past present

carrier pigeons: past & present

petty cash book

serious cash book

cashbooks : a selection

Cash dispenser | A weekend meeting place for townsfolk.

Cash in hand | See Pickpocket.

Castle, Englishman's home is his | Now moated, thanks to climate change.

Casual sex | Now defined as sex for which one does not have to dress up – thereby excluding transvestism, S&M, and rubber and leather fetishes.

Catalogue of errors | See 'Hansard'.

Catchment area | The one time that parents consider geography ahead of maths and English when it comes to choosing their children's schools.

Catchy | Irritating, as in 'What a catchy theme tune'.

Categorical no | The politicians' 'maybe'.

Caterpillar | Archaic. A pre-teen butterfly.

Caution, proceed with | To resume driving after police reprimand.

Cavalry charge | Cost of troop deployment overseas.

Caveat emptor | Latin phrase translating roughly as 'Beware of binmen'.

Ceasefire | A coffee break in Palestine.

Ceiling, glass | 1. Barrier to promotion. 2. Barrier to selling the downstairs flat.

Celebration | Word used solely in the titles of pointless and expensive gift books, as in *Pips! A celebration of the Greenwich Time Signal.*

Celebrity | Anyone who has been on television. Everyone else is a celebrity-in-waiting.

Celebrity, local | A national non-entity.

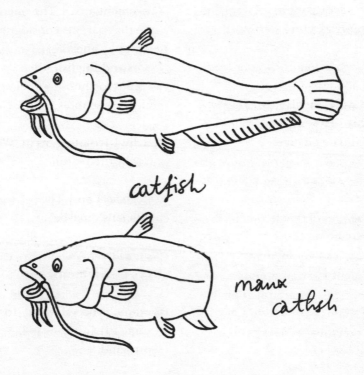

catfish

manx catfish

49

Celibacy | The brief period between any two acts of sexual intercourse.

Cellphone | Mobile smuggled into prison.

Cellulite | The greatest threat facing celebritykind today.

Censorship | 1. A not at all good thing for me or you. 2. A **XXXXXXX** good thing for **XXXXXXXX** you.

Census | A snapshot of the population, i.e. fuzzy, unfocused, and unpleasant to look at.

Centaur | Princess Anne's ideal husband – half man, half horse.

Centigrade | The temperature abroad.

Cereal | A traditional English breakfast – for farm animals.

Ceremony, wedding | A pre-divorce necessity.

Ceremony, without | Co-habiting.

Cert, dead | Any cert that breaks a leg during the Grand National.

Chagrin | French word for gerontophilia.

Chain gang | 1. A collection of criminals. 2. The Tour de France (See 1.)

Chairperson | Correct term for any man or woman in a wheelchair.

Chalk face | Formerly Barbara Cartland, now Wacko Jacko.

Challenge | Vogueish term used to aggrandise any barely difficult task, e.g. The 1 Mile Walkathon Challenge, The Get Up Off The Sofa Challenge, The Say No To Cyanide Challenge.

Chamois | Small leather cloth kept concealed in a window-cleaner's pocket for use in emergencies – such as any householder asking if they have cleaned the windows thoroughly.

Changeable | How TV meteorologists describe weather they cannot predict.

Change for change's sake | See Channel-hopping.

Chaos theory | New theory invented by scientists panicked by the thought that the public were starting to understand the old ones.

Chapbook | Anything by Chris Ryan or Andy McNab.

Character | Estate agents' euphemism for 'old and in need of repair'. Houses with 'bags of character' require purchasers with bags of money.

Charcoal | Semi-combusted fragments of exotic South American or Indonesian trees transported halfway across

Chargers (white): past & present

the world for the purpose of blackening a sausage on a patio in Crewe.

Charity | One of the four Christian virtues. The others are widely thought to be tea, nice places to get married in, and not being Muslim.

Chastity belt | The area of land surrounding a nunnery.

Chat room | A place on the internet where kids can be themselves – and adults can be someone else entirely.

Chattering classes | Result of pupil's lack of respect for teachers.

Chav | A social inferior. According to elitist commentators, the world can be divided into the chavs and chav nots.

Cheek | Self-confidence shown by social inferiors.

Cheerleader | Instruction to crowds in North Korea.

Cheesestrings | A processed food breakthrough. All the

chat room
(English)

chat room
(French)

flavour of cheese with all the nutritional value of string!

Chewing gum | Self-adhesive pavement decoration.

Chicken feed | Other chickens, minced, dried, and pelleted.

Chickenwire | Telegram regretfully informing hen she's tested positive for bird flu.

Childminder | See Television set.

Childproof | Any supposedly impregnable closure a child feels compelled to prove they can open.

Chinchilla | An inadequate beard.

Chinese whispers | 'Hey, mister, you want uncensored internet access?', 'Pro-democracy pamphlets?', 'Remember Tiananmen Square?', etc.

Chintz | The Home Counties version of Bratz dolls. Less bling, more floral fabrics.

Chocoholic | Another name for a chunkard.

Choice | Modern synonym for wealth. The poor have no choice. The rich have too much choice. Most in between choose to accept this.

Christ | An expletive.

Christmas is coming … | First line of children's traditional rhyme, now updated to read: 'Christmas is coming/The goose is getting fatty/Time to rip his liver out/And make it into paté.'

Christmas, old-fashioned | The 'traditional' Victorian-style Christmas to which the poor and homeless are condemned each year.

Church | Quaint disused period building perfect for renovation into recording studios, unique dwelling spaces, etc.

Churchyard | A place where teenagers can smoke undisturbed.

Ciabatta | Lovable *Star Wars* wookie, made with real olive oil.

Cigar, close but no | Air-brushed socially updated photo of Sir Winston Churchill.

Circumstances beyond our control | Circumstances beyond our competence.

Clamp, wheel | Ingenious device for rendering parked cars immobile.

Clapped out | 1. Useless, past it. 2. How national sporting sides are welcomed into their various sporting arenas. After

performing, they are then booed in again. (See 1.)

Class conscious | More likely if schoolchildren have breakfast, apparently.

Class struggle | The teacher's day.

Claustrophobia | Fear of Santa.

Cleanliness | In Richard Dawkins's world, next to godlessness.

Clean shaven | The least suspicious sort of suicide bomber.

Clear blue water | See Chemical toilet.

Clear conscience | Short memory.

Cleavage | The depth to which celebrities will go in order to make the papers.

coat of arms

Clever clogs | Clogs that bought property back in the 1980s.

Climbing frame | An opportunity for legal compensation.

Closed shop | Shop soon to reopen as cybercafé.

Cloud-cuckoo land | A fiercely contested political constituency.

Clubbable | See Seal.

Coat of arms | See Bulletproof vest.

Cocktail | Nowadays a mixture of drugs, none of them alcoholic.

Coconut shy | Allergic to nuts.

Cod | Fish that has had its chips.

Cold call | Apologetic call made to work on Monday morning while firmly pinching one's nose.

Cold comfort | Double choc chip ice cream.

Cold turkey | Boxing day staple.

Colonic irrigation | A crap idea.

Colony | Administrative area where the native population can still get away with blaming another country for their problems.

Combat fatigue | Tired of hearing bad news from Iraq.

Comedian | Anyone the police think is trying to be smart.

Comfrey | Prostitute's one-off special offer.

Commercial traveller | Person who leaves the room during adverts.

Column | A single-authored piece of bigotry in a newspaper. Called a column because it either supports some ridiculous notion or holds up your enjoyment of the rest of the paper.

Coma | A morbid trance-like state similar to normal sleep in that most people are brought out of it by the noise of relatives or pop music.

Common | Rare or threatened, as in common frog, common land, common decency, etc.

Concession | Term used to make a forced climbdown look like an act of generosity.

Concrete proposal | A planning application.

Condensed milk | Mlk.

weddings

funerals

confetti

Confident | Drunk.

Conker | One of the few nuts to which children seem not to be allergic.

Connubial | A married cannibal.

Conservation | Process by which dwindling areas of natural beauty are preserved for future generations to build upon.

Conspicuous consumption | Obvious TB.

Constipation | Also known as 'Reader's block'.

Continental drift | The inexorable move towards Europe.

Contour | Fraudulent package holiday.

Controversial | Media term for one-sided, irresponsible, or ill-researched.

Convenience food | Food so good it shares its title with a public toilet.

Cordless | Every device that comes supplied with a large battery charger and a heavy – but detachable – power cord is said to be cordless.

Cornflakes | Cereal originally developed as a dietary deterrent to masturbation. Ironically, the most famous brand comes in a box displaying a a large cock.

Corniche | The Cornish nouveau riche.

Coronary | Proof that even the most ruthless businessmen are not entirely heartless.

Correspondence | A series of complaining letters to dry-cleaners, the gas-board etc.

Corsair | The air around most building sites.

Cosmology | The study of lettuce.

Cost of living | Climate change.

Cotton | Nature's crude attempt to mimic rayon.

Couch potato | A vegetable.

Council tax | A plague on all our houses.

Counter culture | The social, aesthetic and intellectual aspects of shopping.

Counterfeit | How to be sure it's Heather Mills McCartney.

Courgette Heyer | World's leading author of vegan historical romances.

Courtesy car | Car driven by person not in a hurry.

Coypu | To nervously use a stranger's loo while away from home.

Crash course | 1. Driving lessons. 2. IT lessons.

Crazy | Every idea expressed by a character in an American film that '… Might just work'.

Cream, the cat that got the | The cat that eventually died of coronary arterio-sclerosis.

Creche | A bump to the car in Belgravia.

Credit | Debt.

Critical condition | To be seriously ill in hospital but just well enough to complain about the quality of your treatment.

Croissant | French pastry whose shape is historically based on the Turkish crescent. Its avowed enemy is the hot cross bun. They both de-test the bagel.

Crop circles | Skinheads and their acquaintances.

Croquet | Game based on the legal process. Best enjoyed by the wealthy, one passes through endless hoops, being constantly knocked sideways, before either conceding defeat or losing.

Crossbencher | An angry tramp.

Crucified | Losing six-nil in football.

Cure all | Money.

Curfew | Wading bird that has to be home by six.

Curriculum vitae | 1. A work of fiction. 2. A fiction of work.

Custard pie | A congealed weapon.

Cutting remarks | Banter made by surgeon, usually about golf.

Cyclone | An identical cyclist.

Cypher | Wot Cockney codewords are, guvnor.

D | A tax schedule.

DAB | A modern form of wireless with very heavy power consumption. It stands for Drains All Batteries.

Dad's army | See Fathers for justice.

Daffodils | A sure sign that spring has returned to the petrol station forecourt.

Daily grind | Regular employment in a coffee shop.

Daily paper | Paper publishing corrections on a twenty-four hour rather than a weekly basis

dabhand

Damage to one's reputation | Legal euphemism for hurt pride.

Damp course | Swimming lessons.

Danish blue | 1. Cheese. 2. Porn.

Dark matter | Material believed to make up 90 per cent of the mass of the universe. The other 10 per cent is packaging.

Darling | 1. A favourite. 2. A Chancellor. (See 1.)

Darwin, Charles | Scientist correctly derided for suggesting

daily paper

that all men are descended from less intelligent ancestors, as this seems true only of the most bigoted Creationists.

Dastard | Someone who annoys a ventriloquist.

Data | A plural noun used incorrectly as a single noun by 93.67 per cent of the population, according to the latest datums.

Daughter | In the West, a Miss. In China, a miss.

Dawn chorus | The massed 'goodbye's of London-bound commuters.

Day-Glo | Lurid colours found in nature – on backpackers.

Day in, day out | Scheme to alleviate prison over-crowding.

Dazzling success | A tooth-whitening triumph.

Dead | Not answering one's mobile or responding to emails.

danger money

choking hazard

risk of paper cut

£10 Bank of England 10

flammable

risk of arrest

Deadly sins, seven | Formerly the Christian sins that would guarantee damnation. In the godless modern world they are old age, honesty, technophobia, lack of Ambition, doing things for free, making moral judgements and driving within the speed limit.

Dear Sir or Madam | Start of standard letter to Grayson Perry.

Death bed | See Hospital bed.

Death penalty | Part of the American way of life.

Debacle | A US military strategy.

Decanter | To slow down a horse.

Decay, Urban | Useful process that helps make our countryside look good by comparison.

Deceased | Physically incapable of now dealing with the junk mail they continue to receive.

Decent citizen | Dressed citizen.

Deciduous | Tree with contempt for litter laws.

Decimal point | Point lost on anti-Europeans.

Deckchair | Pioneering form of self-assembly furniture.

Declining years | Time of life when one can successfully decline all invitations to dull events and parties by pretending to be too old and feeble.

Dedicated | Any employee unaware of his full holiday entitlement is said to be dedicated.

Deed, good | A watertight legal document.

Deep and crisp and even | Styles of pizza.

Deep-rooted resentment | See Hedge, leylandii.

Deep thought | Process engaged in by the young when choosing training shoes.

Defeatist | A fan of British tennis.

Defendant | Generally the person in any courtroom in the newest suit.

Defunct | Frequent result of black music being rerecorded by whites.

Déjà vu | The strange feeling you get about eight minutes into watching *Groundhog Day* that you've seen the film somewhere before.

Delegate | Anyone wearing a grey suit at the seaside.

Delicatessen | Shop selling the worst parts of animals more expensively than the cheap bits.

Deluxe | Word used to indicate that a specific sale item has something more than the basic model. However, closer inspection proves this is often little more than the word itself.

Demijohn | Like Richard Littlejohn but only half as bad.

Demo tape | Police VHS of any public protest.

Demur | A doubtful lemur.

Dentist, NHS | Subject of that hilarious music joke: 'What did the woman with one good tooth and one bad tooth say when told she could find an NHS dentist?'... 'Pull the other one!'

demonstration model

Deodorant | Inexact name for what is more accurately a re-odorant – making your armpit smell as fresh as a Warrington chemical factory.

Departed, dearly | The expensively deceased, thanks to inheritance tax.

De rigueur | French for 'I wasted money on this – so should you.'

Derisory | Any sum of money less than one was hoping for is said to be derisory. Any sum of money in excess of expectations – no matter by how much – is merely adequate.

Descriptive passage | The dull part in a novel, thankfully lost in the TV adaptation.

Desert, cultural | Desert with a library and/or arts centre.

Desperate measure | The rod, the chain, the cubit, the ell. I mean, how much more desperate can you get?

Detachable | Synonym for 'easily lost'.

Detailed description | What the police ask for to lull you into thinking they are then going to do something.

Détente | Term implying a state of improving relations between potentially antagonistic countries. Curiously, the word comes from the French.

Devil | Mythical evil being that used to drive people into church, and nowadays draws them into the cinema.

Diagnosis | A medicated guess.

Diagram | Strippagram dressed like the late Princess Di.

Diamond Jubilee | Celebration of sixty years of not having your jewellery stolen.

Diatonic | View not shared by the Duke of Edinburgh.

Dictionary | Book with a beginning, a middle, and an end – but never in that order.

Dictum | What George Best did to beauty queens.

Didgeridoo | A mournful tube. See also Northern Line.

Die out | To collapse on the patio.

Dietary fibre | Having the courage and strength not to eat cream cakes.

Diffident | Elizabethan dissident.

Dig | 1950s slang enjoying a revival. It is commonly acceptable to say you 'dig' music, horror movies, Bansky, etc. It is less acceptable to reveal you dig cesspits, graves, or badgers.

Digital camera | Device that has revolutionised home photography in that it is now possible to store thousands of unviewed bad snaps on a PC rather than in shoeboxes.

Digital clock | Timepiece accurate to one second a decade but impossible to read in daylight.

Dignified silence | Yet to think of a suitable comeback.

Dim view, take a | Use camera indoors without flash.

Diminishing returns | One of the few laws global businesses still fully respect.

Dim sum | Way to save money on lighting.

Dining car | Vehicle belonging to any person with children. The wrappers on the floor attest to its use.

Dire consequences | Duller than usual party game.

Direct mail | Mail that goes directly into the bin.

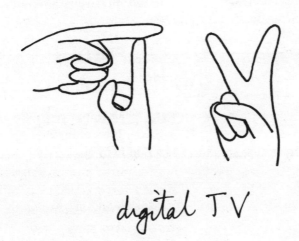

digital TV

Dirty dancing | Cromwellian view of Morris-dancing.

Disabled toilet | Vandalised toilet.

Disappointment, big | Any small disappointment when recounted in a letter of complaint.

Discerning customer | Marketing term used to flatter the wealthier potential purchaser who cannot actually discern that they're being manipulated.

Discotheque | A forcing-ground for mime artists.

Discreet | To keep judiciously quiet about others' misuse of the word 'discrete'.

Discretion | The boring part of valour.

Dish the dirt | To serve school dinners.

Dish, satellite | TV aerial that blends effortlessly with domestic architecture by looking like a bird bath skewered to the side of the house by a drunk using an umbrella.

Diva | Word used to excuse any foul tempered female singer. My advice, liva.

Disposable income | The money we throw away on rubbish.

Distinct | No longer smelly.

Diversion | An indirect approach to roadworks.

Divine right | Quality possessed by royalty and footballers.

Division of labour | Woman screams. Man takes photos.

domestics : past & present

Divorce | A post-nuptial agreement.

DIY | A precursor to DYI – Do Yourself Injury.

DNA database | Police records of the genetic identity of thousands of Britons, whether convicted or not. DNA stands for *D*eoxyribose*N*ucleic *A*cid or, if you're one of the innocent, Done Naff All.

Dog tired | Tired, but still capable of barking all night long.

Doggy bag | Receptacle for taking home Korean restaurant leftovers.

Dolphins, swimming with | Claimed to be a positive life-enhancing experience despite the cost, the constant fake smile, and the fishy breath. For a cheaper alternative, try a trip to the local pool with any sushi-loving Scientologist.

Domain name | For more information go to www. asksomespottykid.com.

Doner kebab? | Post-closing-time question. The safest answer is donwoner kebab.

Dotted line, signing on the | A dashed mistake.

Double decker | Rare opportunity for bus users to look down on motorists.

Double glazing | Ingenious system for trapping the merest amount of condensation between two panes of glass. Luckily it also affords effective sound insulation, so no one outside your home can hear you being annoyed about it.

Double standards | The standard standards.

Doughnut | Cake with fat-free centre.

Down market | The global trade in goosefeathers.

Drainpipe trousers | Rumoured to be a remedy for water on the knee.

Drive | 1. Burning ambition. 2. Burning fossil fuels.

Driving instructor | Usually the eldest in a group of joy riders.

Driving range | Legally, 17 to 70. Starts much younger on many estates.

Droop, brewer's | Dispiriting side-effect of drinking: a glans half-empty.

Druid | Lib Dem with access to Stonehenge.

Dry-cleaning | An offshoot of the wire coat-hanger industry.

Dual carriageway | Frustrating road for many motorists, lacking a middle lane to hog.

Dumb waiter | Waiter yet to twig the link between their tip and the pretence of co-operation.

Dumpling | Any small item abandoned in a layby.

Dundee | We have now.

BRINN GG!

Yah! Hello?

ear-rings: past & present

E | 1. Chemical added to food. 2. Chemical added to teenagers.

Eager beaver | Beaver still in first weeks of new job.

Ear | A headphone socket.

Early bird | Bird clearly not dependent on public transport.

Early English | Mama, Dada, Burga.

Early music | See Neighbours, inconsiderate.

Earplug | Advert in podcast.

Ears, all | The cheaper sort of pork sausages.

Ears are burning, my | Result of answering phone while ironing.

Earth, down to | Quality valued in: 1. People; 2. Aliens.

Earth Mother | A mudda.

Earthly use, of no | Document informing holder that star CX12YR3201 in the constellation Andromeda has been registered in their name. Happy Birthday.

Earthwork | Environmentalism.

EastEnders | A harrowingly realistic portrayal of life on a film set in Elstree.

Easter | A national celebration of chocolate.

Easterly | Anything with eggs, chicks or ducklings on it.

Easy chair | Budget furniture company. However, the seats have hardly any leg-room and cannot be reserved. Cushions cost extra.

Easy meat | Mince.

Eau-de-nil | French for a no-score draw.

Eavesdropping? | Call 0800-GUTTERBUSTERS now!

Eco-friendly | The only cars the hedgehogs forgive.

E.coli | Environmentally conscious pathogen.

Ecstasy | Drug which causes short-term euphoria and long-term memory loss – which its advocates tend to forget.

Edge, cutting |
Any of the four sides of any seemingly innocent piece of A4 paper.

Edible | Word used to alert fools to the possibility of swallowing cake decorations, underwear, condoms, etc.

Editing | Process by which the works of JK Rowling are reduced to a size and weight a child can actually lift.

Editor, newspaper | A future ex-newspaper editor.

Editorial | An opinion of such importance it occupies less space than the daily cartoon but is often more ridiculous.

Education, education, education | See Promises, promises.

Education, private | An education parents pay for.

Education, sex | The only set of lessons children can see as being still relevant to them after they've left school.

Education, state | An education society pays for.

Eel | 1. To be sick in Spain. 2. To get better in east London.

Eerie silence | Any silence nowadays.

Effects, personal | One's possessions. Not to be confused with Personal FX – farting, belching, etc.

Effects, special | A plot substitute.

Effing | A vulgar forest.

Egg | The chicken's contribution to political debate.

common eel

conga eels

Eggshells, walking on | Qualifying test for waif-like catwalk models.

Ego trip | A record-breaking journey made by Richard Branson.

Eight, one over the | Taxing maths problem for the drunken teen.

Eighteen certificate | Film which minors are unable to watch at the cinema, so they watch it at home on DVD instead.

Elbow grease | About the only grease shunned by the obese.

Election, general or local | Rare opportunity for parents to learn the location of their children's school.

Electoral register | List of people happy to give their address to junk mail distributors.

Electric blanket | Supplementary warmth for the non-cat or dog owner.

Electric chair | A not quite final resting place.

Electrocardiogram | A picture of health.

Elephant in the room | Hazard of over-zealous rodent control.

Elf | Any Tolkien character with a name reminiscent of an indigestion medicine, e.g. Galadriel, Minel, Rumil, etc.

Elixir | See Cunnilingus.

Elizabeth II | The world's most famous state-supported parent of problem children.

Elm | Tree conspicuous by its absence.

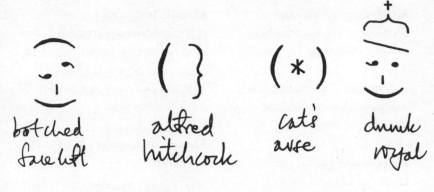

botched face lift

altred hitchcock

cat's arse

drunk royal

emotions, underused

Eloquent | Description of any politician able to use an autocue.

Email | The last post for letter-writing.

Emancipation | A woman who behaves as badly as a man is said to be emancipated.

Embarrassment of riches | Tax avoidance difficulties.

Embassy, American | Building that puts the 'flag' into 'conflagration'.

Emigrant | Another man's immigrant.

Eminent | 1. Adjective available to professionals wishing to bump up their fees. 2. Word used to introduce any academic no one has heard of before. If the academic is retired or close to death, they are elevated to 'pre-eminent'.

Emissary | Cross between an emu and a cassowary.

Emotional wreck | The RMS *Titanic*.

Empathy | The shared understanding between two people on the same pay grade.

Employee of the month | Award most hotly contested in February.

Emulsifier | Chemical added to food and paint.

Enamel | Old-fashioned finish for teeth, now superseded by metal and plastic.

Encumber | To adorn with cucumbers.

Encyclopaedias, set of | System for collecting dust in alphabetical order.

End all wars, the war to | The next one, honest.

Endless nightmare | The M25.

Endosperm | Result of too-tight trousers.

English as a foreign language | American.

English breakfast, full | A cooked meal consisting of eggs from France, Danish bacon and Irish sausages, washed down with lashings of tea (Kenya).

English reserve | Homegrown Premier League player.

Enjoy | Americanism encountered increasingly often in the UK, implying the phrase 'Enjoy it'. Suitable truncated responses might include 'Shove', 'Drop' and 'Shut'.

Enough is enough | Statement contradicted by the equally common claim that 'less is more', but 'you can't have too much of a good thing'. Confusingly, all are true.

Ensconced | Partway through a Cornish cream tea.

En suite | Any hotel bedroom separated by only a thin door from a permanently dripping showerhead is said to have all the benefits of being en suite.

Enterprising | Opportunistic.

Entertainment, pure | An embattled concept in a world dominated by edutainment, dramedy and infomercials. Most of them are compollocks.

Envelope | A jealous antelope.

Epic | Any film so unnecessarily long that one has to go out and urinate during it.

Epidemic | The rapid and uncontrollable spread of any contagious disease through all the newspapers.

Epitaph | The one bit of Karl Marx that people still read.

Equal airtime | Broadcasting principle in which all political

parties are given an identical opportunity to irritate voters.

Equal opportunities | Freedom for all people, regardless of race, creed, colour or wealth, to be as bad as each other.

Erotic | Word used to describe any material that's not quite pornographic enough.

Escort | 1. A prostitute with knowledge of the theatre. 2. Car named after British top-shelf publication. See also the Ford Fiesta, the Mini Mayfair, the Austin Razzle, and the Vauxhall Havaleer.

Eskimos | Indigenous people with no commercially adaptable music and lacking in exciting new cuisine ideas.

Essex | The taxi drivers' homeland.

Estate agent | Salesman guilty of a sin of commission, and evidence for the claim that the devil is in the details.

Estimate | A rare occasion for modesty in workmen.

Etcetera | Device used by journalists to indicate a lack of research, e.g. 'There were many great deaf composers – Beethoven, etc.'

Ethnic look | Healthy, well-fed white people wearing beads are said to have an ethnic look.

Euphemism | Word used by those without the courage to be crude.

Europe | A group of disparate nations united by a common resentment of the Swiss.

European ideal | A German washing machine, plumbed in by a Pole, laundering some Italian clothes, while British pop music drowns out the sound of a French couple arguing.

European Union | The only union the government still has to listen to.

Euthanasia | A way of putting old people out of their family's misery.

Evangelical | Word meaning bothersome.

Eve | The world's first victim of high-pressure selling.

eve

christmas eve

Even-handed | Possessing two or four hands.

Every good boy deserves favour | But it's the bad ones who get the attention.

Exclusion | Curious policy of denying access to school for a child who clearly doesn't want to be there.

Exaggeration, no | Some exaggeration.

Exchange, heated | Any customer-complaints call centre.

Excretion | A former Greek islander.

Exercise book | Opportunistic volume brought out by seemingly every TV presenter who ever had a baby or shed one or two pounds.

Exercise, military | Bending over backwards to not upset the Americans. Or the Russians. Or the Chinese. Or the French.

Exit, no | Sign placed conveniently by the shortest way out of a tube station.

Exodus, mass | The movement of people away from the church.

Experience | Word used to make ordinary museums sound more interesting. For example, the Burton upon Trent Museum of Brewing and Allied Trades becomes the Bitter Experience, the Isle of Wight Cultural Heritage Centre becomes the Jimi Hendrix Experience.

Exploratory surgery | Surgery to reveal the eventual cost of treatment.

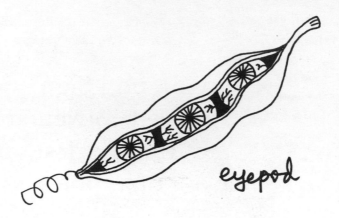

eyepod

Express service | Proper service compared to the speed of normal service.

Extinct | Biological term meaning once-edible or once-decorative.

Extracurricular | Scholastic euphemism for 'extra-cost'.

Extraordinary | Anything ordinary described by a children's TV presenter.

Extraordinary likeness | Any official portrait of the Queen that actually looks like her.

Estimated time of arrival | Optimistic time of arrival.

Extrovert | Any person who is loud even when sober.

F | 1. Newspaper prefix to any row of asterisks.
2. Formerly a temperature, now a word.

FA | A sweet nothing.

Fabric of society | Denim.

Facebook | An internet site linking people with a shared interest: themselves.

Facelift | Surgical procedure which leaves recipients grinning from ear to ear. Often literally.

Face value | The boost to a magazine's circulation from putting a a celeb on the cover.

Fact | An internet rumour.

Fact-finding tour | The long journey one undergoes in the attempt to locate a still-operating public library.

DO NOT
IRON

DO NOT
FOLD

DO NOT
HANG

DO NOT
PUT AWAY

MUM WASH
ONLY

fabric care symbols: a teenager's guide

Facts of life | The birds and the bees, and the birds and the birds, and the bees and the bees.

Faction | A blend of fact and fiction. See also Biography, authorised.

Fag break | The Oatesian moment for the twenty-first century. 'I'm just going outside. I may be some time, cough, cough.'

Fahrenheit | Archaic temperature scale that had the pleasing effect of making the British summer seem hotter.

Fair, all the fun of the | 1. What blondes have. 2. The sheer joy of forking over twenty or thirty quid in the pursuit of a cankerous goldfish or a giant inflatable alien.

Fair-minded | Obsessed with rollercoasters.

Fair play | Even-handed cheating.

Fairy godmother | Fictional godparent who – like a real godparent – exists solely to furnish gifts rather than provide religious guidance.

Fairy lights | A blinking nuisance.

Fairy tale ending | Being chopped to pieces by a woodman.

Fair tale romance | Story where the prince and princess live happily ever after, after their divorce.

False alarm | Dummy box placed on house to deter burglars.

False economy | Cheap flight that takes you not to Dubrovnik but a distant airfield in a town with a name like Myelzout, thereby costing you a bus ride and a morning in the process.

Family, happy | Family of no interest to TV documentary-makers.

Family size | Marketing method used to promote larger, better value packs of many commodities, with the obvious exception of condoms.

FAQs | Frequently asked questions. Not to be confused with TFAQs – too frequently asked questions. These include: Do you need help packing? Have you got a loyalty card? Do you want cashback? Are you in the carpark?

Farcical | A small piece of frozen farce.

Farewell concert | Often an occasion for false optimism.

Far-fetched | Any strawberry on sale in January.

Farmer | A man viewed quite differently by the public and the supermarkets. He either tills the soil, or soils the tills.

Farm house | Country dwelling of TV celebrities, writers, sportsmen, etc.

Fascism | Philosophy which set out to dominate the world, but had to settle for dominating TV history channels.

Fashionable | Any idea, practice or style specially designed to look stupid in a few years' time.

Fashion victim | Some poor child in an overseas sweat shop.

Fashionably late | To be buried in Manolo Blahniks.

Fast food | Food delivered promptly because it isn't worth waiting for.

Fat chance | The likelihood of sticking to any faddy diet.

Fate | Excuse for things going wrong. Any success is due to either luck or sheer hard work, depending on the degree of envy it generates.

Fatherland | Enterprising theme park catering for Saturday dads and their kids. In an ironic reversal, mothers are denied access.

Fauna | To be ever so slightly browner.

Fawn | Fashion term used to make brown sound trendy.

Fearless | 1. Drunk. 2. Stupid.

Features, bonus | Characteristic of : 1. DVDs; 2. Picasso portraits.

Feet and inches | Just two of the measures taken by Brussels.

Feline | Adjective used to imply the graceful, agile movements of cats rather than scratching furniture or defecating in flowerbeds.

Fellow feeling | Now punishable with a caution.

Fellowship of the Ring | The boxing fraternity.

Feminism | Creed of equality, as a result of which women stand up for women, and men on buses no longer do.

Fence-sitting | Ability shared by MPs and cats. Other shared talents include sleeping long periods, attention-seeking, shifting loyalties, and licking arseholes.

Feng shui | A way of channelling energy – most frequently into the moving of heavy furniture.

past   present

female impersonators: past & present

Fern | Leafy plant growing wild in the foyers of modern office blocks.

Ferret | Domesticated polecat rumoured to be lesbian as only ever seen in trousers.

Fertiliser | 1. What the autopsy showed Dodi didn't do to Di. 2. The lurid newspaper claims that he did.

Fete | Obligatory crime scene for any English TV detective series with a rural setting.

Fettle | Word never seen in public without the adjective 'fine'.

Fevered imagination | Handy talent for bird flu headline writers.

Fewer | Word used by lesser writers fewer times than 'less' though 'fewer' is more accurate and 'less' less applicable more or less always.

Fibreboard | Long-overdue new name for the Colonic Roughage Awareness Panel.

Fiddle | An instrument of business.

Fiddle, fit as a | Lacquered, but scraping by. Bowed, but unbeaten.

Fidelity | A constant problem.

Field trip | Result of ingesting the wrong type of mushrooms.

Fig | The standard British unit of care for the elderly.

Fight or flight | The main options available to drunken football fans in airports.

Figurine | The great new fat-free spread! Marge for the large!

Film of the book | Film of some of the book.

Finishing school | What kids soon won't get to do until they're 18.

Fir | Tree which keeps its leaves all year round except during Christmas.

Fire alarm | Bell rung to allow employees to stand outside and smoke.

Firearm | Result of brushing coat with sparkler.

Firefighter | A non-gender-specific public hero. Er…

First strike | Indefensible defence option.

Fish and chips | Meal unpopular with the young – being only fifty per cent chips.

Fish finger | Digital food.

Fit to bust | Basic instructions for the first-time bra-buyer.

Five | The lowest denomination of cocaine applicator.

Fixed smile | Outcome of expensive dentistry.

Fixture, sporting | Cheating.

Flagpole, see who salutes it; run it up the | ...Imprison the rest'. (North Korean proverb)

Flame, old | A spent match.

Flamingo | Bird spared endless speculation about what colour to paint the nursery.

Flapjack | A male flapjill.

Flares | A seventies leg-end.

Flatfish | The only pets allowed in swanky apartments.

Flavour of the month | Cinnamon. It is always cinnamon.

Flea | Tiny, jumping, blood-sucking parasite, which if it were the size of a man would be in financial services.

Fleshpot | See Paté.

Flight attendant | Cabin crew member whose on-board weight allowance is largely taken up by the make-up they are wearing.

flatfish

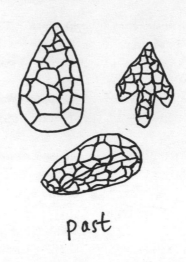

past

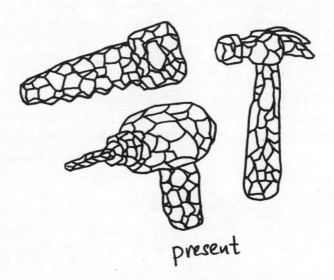

present

flint tools: past & present

Flip-flop | Poorly received boardroom presentation.

Floor, take the | Next move after stealing church roof.

Flop | A West End show with actors not known from television.

Flow, go with the | Great advice since the days of Noah.

Flower of Scotland | Thistle, deep-fried.

Flushed with pride | Any water-saving eco-friendly reed-bed loo.

Fly-fishing | Pastime requiring great patience, but all things comes to he who wades.

Flying doctor | House doctor on amphetamines to get through three-day shift.

Foam at the mouth | Post-cappuccino hazard.

Foie gras | Distastefully made food product, subject of the festive rhyme: 'Christmas is coming, The goose is getting fatty; Time to rip its liver out And make it into pate.'

"WATER LEVELS ARE STILL RISING, ELECTRICITY IS STILL NOT AVAILABLE..."

flood light

fat-free!   sugar-free!   low salt!

food labelling for idiots

Foist | A first for Brooklyn, NY.

Folk music | The delightful simple tunes of any country except one's own.

Follicle | A small folly.

Food additive | Excess packaging.

Foolproof | Any system which only intelligent people can ruin is said to be foolproof.

Football | A religion – akin to Judaism because it traditionally happens on Saturdays.

Footpath, public | A way to annoy a farmer.

Force of habit | A platoon of nuns.

Forecast, weather | See Judgement, clouded.

Forgetfulness |

Forthcoming attractions | Imminent disappointments.

Fortitude | The courage needed to admit to being 40.

Fortune-teller | Mystic gifted

with such amazing powers that they are always capable of gaining employment with a funfair.

Fox-hunting | A fox followed by hounds followed by huntsmen followed by protestors followed by the police. Hence hunting is called a country pursuit.

Fracas | Elegant French term for a fistfight outside a boozer.

Freebie | Gift usually worth exactly what you paid for it.

Free house | A City bonus.

French cricket | Like English cricket but with better-dressed players.

French toast | 'Couchez les Anglais!'

Fresco | The French Tesco.

Fresh | Any item within its use by date is claimed to be fresh. One second past this, and it must then be destroyed.

past

present

free spirits: past & present

Friction-powered | 1. Toys.
2. The EU.

Friday | Saturday-lite.

Friday night | Friday from lunchtime onwards.

Friendly fire | Tragic proof of faults on both sides.

Fritter | To be even more frightened.

Fuck off | A cancelled assignation.

Full moon | Moon about 2070 given current population growth.

Fuller figure | Fashion writer's term for the next size up from malnutrition.

Fundamentalism | Religious extremism espoused by preachers talking through their fundaments.

Fun run | Unusual event in which people run through city streets without police in pursuit.

Fur | Coating found on:
1. The outside of animals;
2. The inside of arteries.

Future-proof | Dead.

G | 1. A force of nature. 2. A spot of romance.

Gadget, ingenious | Any device whose use will eventually recoup the time lost in figuring out how to make it work.

Gaia | Concept of earth as one super-organism. Sadly, the future of Gaia looks pretty daia.

Galore | Very few – as in 'bargains galore', 'savings galore', etc.

Gamble | To travel by public transport.

Gamekeeper | Teacher keen on confiscating pupils' hand-held consoles.

Gannet | Bird with food issues.

Garage | 1. Place where households keep their most valued possession: the freezer. 2. The largest single room in any modern new-build.

Garbage in, garbage out | 1. A computing truism. 2. British youth custody policy. 3. The effect of tides in British coastal waters. 4. The electoral system of parliamentary democracy.

Garble | To gargle incoherently.

Garden | A decking opportunity.

Garden, indoor | A cannabis factory.

Garden birds | Rachel de Thame, Kim Wilde, Charlie Dimmock, etc.

Garden centre | The modern church. Open every Sunday and good for the soul.

Garden of rest | Garden concreted over to save on lawn-mowing.

gateway drug

doorway drug

Gas chamber | See Commons, House of.

Gascon | Any too-good-to-be-true deal from an energy supplier.

Gas mask | A plug-in air freshener.

Gastronomy | Science which rhymes with 'astronomy' but has little else in common bar Stargazey Pie.

Gate-crasher | Inconsiderate postman.

Gates, heaven's | One of the few places rumoured still to employ friendly and welcoming door staff.

Gavel | How judges attract the public's attention, in addition to passing ludicrous sentences and revealing their idiot opinions to the press.

Gear change | Dull mechanical operation from whose tyranny the motorist has been freed by the development of the traffic jam.

Generalisation | Best avoided on the whole.

General practitioner | Any doctor with whom one is registered in a group practice. So called because you generally end up seeing someone else.

Generally speaking | Specifically waffling.

Genesis | 1. A pop group. 2. The first book of the Bible. Amazingly for such a best-selling book, no one has yet brought out a prequel.

Geneva Convention | A free Swiss holiday for businessmen.

Genius | 99% perspiration. 1% inspiration.

Genius, marketing | 99% perspiration. 1% inspiration. 0% artificial colours or flavourings. Fat free!

Gentlemen's agreement | A drug deal conducted in a men's lavatory.

Gentrification | Process by which middle-class people transform a run-down, scruffy area by filling it with scaffolding, skips and building rubble.

Geriatric | Any person who can recall their youth but can't tell you the name of the current Prime Minister. This is a particularly cruel test in Italy.

Getaway, quick | Any getaway not involving baggage.

Gherkin | A skyscraper-shaped fruit.

Ghost | The dress size below size zero.

Ghoul | Term of abuse for any person who pays attention to badly injured people in the street rather than one who pays money to see them in the cinema.

Giant panda | Reclusive creature, half black, half white, noted for its reproductive peculiarities. See also Jackson, Michael.

Gigolo | Like a pedalo, but costlier to hire and potentially more exhausting.

Gingko | Chinese tree used in medicine to improve thingummybob.

Gipsies | Itinerant folk that tow caravans along the roads and then wonder why people dislike them.

Gipsy moth | Moth with unfounded reputation for stealing other moths' caterpillars.

Give and take | 1. Latitude. 2. Ironically, given 1, the two main associations with the word 'offence'.

Glacier | A frozen asset best not liquidated for the sake of coast-dwellers.

Gloat | An arrogant goat.

Glockenspiel | School percussion instrument, frequently confused with the xylophone. However, only the xylophone can be completely destroyed by fire.

Gloucester, double | Cheese so good they named it twice.

Go-slow | Accelerated work rate for British railway ticket clerks.

Go, touch and | Public transport term applicable to: 1. Oystercard users; 2. Rush-hour gropers.

Goblet | A small mouth.

God-awful | Richard Dawkins's chances of salvation.

Godfather | A man of many parts. Parts I and II being the best.

Golden handshake | A pre-trousering post-urination flourish.

Golf | Game played by men who will walk 600 yards in all weathers to put a small white ball in a hole but can't put a sock in a laundry basket.

Gooseberry | Grape currently saving for electrolysis.

Gore, Kensington | The result of running over a poodle outside Barker's.

Gorgeous | Any topless newspaper model whose first name begins with a G is said to be gorgeous.

Goujon | A fish finger with a college education.

Gourd | 1. A Cockney deity. 2. A Whitehall deity.

Graduate | 1. A credit to his family. 2. A huge debt to the bank.

Graffiti | The work of a bunch of aerosols.

Granary bread | Bread recommended as good for the bowels by doctors, and good for business by dentists.

grammar school

non-grammar school

Grandfather clock | A clock nowadays often no more than thirty years old.

Granivorous | Eats old ladies.

Granny flat | Consequence of being unable to outpace steamroller.

Graph paper | The *FT* or *The Economist.*

Grasp of politics | Taxation.

Grass widow | Neglected partner of persistent cannabis user.

Gratuitous sex and violence | Sex and violence demanded by the public rather than the plot.

Grave | Elvis's cunning hiding place.

Gravity | Force acting on all bodies, to the delight of cosmetic surgeons.

Grey squirrel | A red menace.

Gridlocked | Unable to complete a Sudoku.

GSOH, must have | Request which is fine in Lonely Hearts ads but should ring alarm bells when encountered in the property pages.

Guantanamo Bay detainee | An unindicted guest.

Guesswork | The sound economic principle behind the management of your private pension money

Guilt trip | 1. The twice yearly visit to church. 2. Any carbon-costly flight.

Gull | Bird whose haunting cry brings a touch of romance to every landfill.

Gunpowder Plot | One of the few conspiracies yet to be linked to the CIA.

Gutted | The disappointment felt by soccer players and herrings.

Guy Fawkes | Religious fundamentalist terrorist – complete with beard, knowledge of explosives and overseas military training – noted for being executed more effectively than his plot.

hairdo

hairdon't

H | A type of bomb. So called because it would be awful to drop it.

Hackle | A small journalist.

Hackney carriage | 1. Police car. 2. Ambulance. 3. Hearse.

Haggis | Scottish delicacy that is the food equivalent of Russian dolls: minced stomach, cooked in a stomach, that ends up in a stomach.

Hail | The kindest interpretation of any lumps of ice that fall from the sky in the vicinity of a flight-path.

Hairdresser | A part-time travel consultant.

Half-arsed | See Builder's bum. (Or, rather, don't if you can avoid it.)

Half-mast | Mobile phone transmitter following local residents' protests.

Hallmark | Damage caused by bicycle storage.

Halloween | Annual celebration in which, thanks to trick or treat, gangs of children go from door to door imposing themselves on householders in a way previously employed by Jehovah's Witnesses.

Halo | Like the bowler, a now obsolete item of headgear.

Ham | Incurably bad actor.

Hamlet | 1. A play. 2. A small cigar. (Only the former can still be enjoyed indoors.)

Hammock | One of the few beds people still might find it hard to jump into.

Hand, old | Clue to the real age of seemingly timeless actresses.

hard water

Handgun | The largest size of firearm that will fit comfortably into a schoolbag.

Handle, too hot to | Any pastry-based snack after heating in a microwave. It will also be too soggy to handle.

Handmade | 1. A ridiculously expensive British object. 2. A ridiculously cheap third world object.

Hand-me-downs | The Orb, the Sceptre, the Imperial Crown, etc.

Hands-on experience | Unwarranted consequence for many women of travel in crowded lifts and trains.

Hand-to-mouth existence | Living on a diet of beefburgers.

Happy | Ignorant of the true facts of the situation.

Hard-and-fast | Rules of engagement for would-be male porn stars.

cream horn

turnover

croissant-neuf

hardcore danish pastries

Hard drive | Any car journey undertaken while simultaneously attempting to steer and eat a kebab.

Hard lens | Contact lens easier to locate when mislaid than a soft lens as it produces a distinctive crunching sound underfoot.

Hard shoulder | Children's linear urinal.

Hare Krishna movement | Walking up and down Oxford street with a shaved head and a cymbal.

Hasty decision | Accusation yet to be levelled at the legal process.

Haul | The insignificant quantity of drugs or ammunition collected as a result of some massive police operation is called a haul.

Hazard, potential | Anything small enough for a child to put in its mouth is a potential hazard. Nowadays this includes much of its food.

Headbanger | 1. A long-haired, nodding rock fan. 2. An unwary, poorly anchored bendy-bus passenger.

Head over heels in love | Advanced intercourse position.

Health food | Any food not yet proven to be harmful.

Health warning, government | Proof of the ineffectiveness of truth in advertising.

Hearse | The only slow-moving vehicle in an area free from speed cameras.

Heart | Organ vital for circulating alcohol, nicotine and cholesterol round the body.

Heather, lucky white | 1. Plant conferring good fortune on apparently everyone except those reduced to pressing it upon the public in the street. 2. The former Mrs McCartney.

Heavy metal | Leaden music.

Heavy petting | Keeping elephants.

Hectare | Charmless metric unit of area whose only resemblance to 'the acre' is purely anagrammatical.

Hedgehog | The only creature etiquette permits to drink from a saucer.

Heedless | A decapitated Scot.

Heightened security | Taller policemen.

Hell | 1. Other people. 2. Other people's children. 3. Concept dismissed by modern theologians who do not travel by public transport.

Hell-bent | Fundamentalist view of homosexuality.

Hemline | The confidential telephone counselling service for distressed dressmakers.

Her Majesty's Stationery Office | The country's leading publisher of horror and fantasy titles.

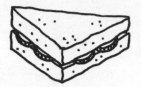

cucumber sandwich

hash cake

high teas: past & present

Heritage industry | An opportunity for unemployed miners to pretend to be Victorian colliers.

Hermit | Tabloid description of any celebrity unwilling to be continually featured in the papers.

Heroes, land fit for | A graveyard.

Hibernation | Nature's way of avoiding Christmas television.

High and dry | The two main categories of drug-user.

Highbrow | 1. Result of extensive academic reading. 2. Result of extensive cosmetic surgery.

High seas | All seas in about 50 years' time.

Hijack | Potential aviation hazard useful for taking the nervous flier's mind off the possibility of crashing.

Hindleg | Donkey limb at risk from exposure to politicians.

Hindsight | See Builder's bum, again.

hippo campus

Historic occasion | Any event so momentous that a souvenir mug is issued.

History | Repeats itself.

History channel | Repeats itself every 4 hours.

Hitch, technical | A geek wedding.

Hobson's choice | A political alternative.

Home and dry | Just returned from a spell in the Priory.

Homesickness | Result of overuse of plug-in air fresheners.

Honourable member | Rare example of the amusing use of sarcasm.

Hook, Captain | Seaman forced into criminality by government failure to protect the value of Invalidity Benefit.

Hops | Lager-flavoured plants.

Horror movies | Michael Winner's home videos.

Horseless carriage | Carriage unwisely left unattended outside French butchers.

Horse sense | The royal substitute for intelligence.

Hot | The non-functioning tap in a public convenience.

Houdini | Early exponent of thinking outside the box.

Human resources | Now known simply as HR, thereby dispensing with the services of 12 superfluous letters. These will be offered retraining.

Humorist | Dull writer incapable of having straightforward encounters with appliances, tradesmen and public servants.

Hunchback | Small family car popular with Parisian bell-ringers.

Hunger strike | An attempt to effect change by going without food. Yet to be proven successful in Africa.

Hunter-gatherers | Prehistory's first people with a double-barrelled name.

Hypnosis | The one way remaining to get people to do things without the offer of payment.

Hypocaust | Early Roman attempt to add value to their homes.

I | Letter overused by: 1. Apple Computers; 2. Newspaper columnists; 3. Carmen Miranda.

Iambic pentameter | Elizabethan attempt at the complexities of rap music lyrics.

Ibis | The new internet-ready biscuit from Apple.

Ice | Substance known to mathematicians and chemists as $(H_2O)^3$.

Icecap | Cap available each year in smaller and smaller sizes.

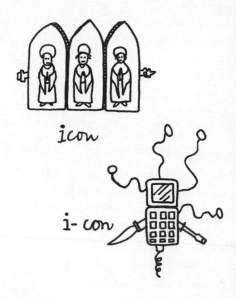

icon

i- con

ibis ibid.

Icepack | Collective noun for climatologists.

Iconoclast | Self-description of any teenager who hates everything but owns a dictionary.

ID | The key tool in the sinister plot to keep the makers of coin-operated photo booths in profit for years to come.

ID parade | Succession of teenagers in a socially responsible off-licence.

Idea, bad | Deer with conjunctivitis.

Ideal home | Same home as the one you have now, but worth what it will be in 20 years' time.

Identity theft | Pretending to be someone you aren't. To date, the biggest offender is Rory Bremner.

Idiosyncracy | Any fault in a friend as described to a stranger.

If | Poem encountered first at school then 30 years later at a funeral.

Igloo | Inuit home now with serious damp problem.

Ignoramus | Latin. To refuse to notice a small rodent.

Ignorance | No defence in law, unless you're a judge.

Ilk | Evaporated milk.

Ill-assorted | An incongruous mixture, not be confused with Ill (Assorted), the daily fodder of the general practitioner.

Ill-fated | Synonymous with 'invented by Clive Sinclair'.

Ill-gotten gains | Treasury view of inherited wealth.

Illiterate | Person whose lack of literary skills will confine them to menial jobs such as chalking up the menus in pubs and writing market traders' signs.

implants

eggplants

Illuminati | Aggrandising nickname for the people of Blackpool.

Illustrated, fully | 1. Any maximally tattooed body part. 2. The Argos catalogue.

Image conscious | What modern politicians have to be. Hence few of them appear in public with their pants actually on fire.

Imitation leather | Fabric chosen by life-revering sado-masochists.

Immaterial | Facts which annoyingly disprove expert theory are said to be immaterial.

Immemorial, time | For the over-50s, any appointment not actually written down.

Immigrant, illegal | See Immigrant penniless'.

Immigration | Major topic of conversation among ex-pat Brits lacking a sense of irony.

Immoral earnings | Rational view of City bonuses.

Impala | Blood-thirsty African antelope, the most notorious example being Vlad the Impala.

Impartial | 1. Any referee who favours one's own team is said to be impartial. 2. Belgian. 3. Too foolish to recognise a bribe.

Impatient | Any person rapidly angered by their circumstances is said to be impatient, hence the word is frequently interchangeable with 'inpatient'.

Impeccable references | References concocted by the applicant themselves.

Imperial | Term applying nowadays to soap and peppermints.

Impromptu performance | Newspaper euphemism for any long-planned display imposed by egotistical performers on party guests.

Improvements, home | Getting the children to leave.

Impunity | The rallying cry of the National Alliance of Satanic Workers and Allied Demons (NASWAD).

Inaccessible | Not accessible by car.

Inanimate object | Animate object placed in front of TV set.

Inaudible | The voice of reason.

Inbreeding | Process discouraged in all beasts except royalty.

In-car entertainment | Criticising other road-users. Not be confused with Inca entertainment – pan pipes.

Incarceration | The jailing of the middle class. Working classes are banged up.

Incest | Sexual relations.

Inch | Pre-decimal measure which, curiously, has been retained in Britain almost solely for the assessment of erogenous body parts.

Incipient baldness | Advanced baldness cunningly disguised.

Incision | The only politically acceptable NHS cut.

Incommunicado | Unable to communicate with others, i.e. in a railway tunnel.

Incompetent | Due for promotion.

Inconclusive | Said of any test with embarrassing results.

Incorruptible | Independently wealthy.

Incurable disease | Any curable disease with a prohibitively expensive treatment.

Indecision | A sometimes OK thing. Probably.

Indefatigable | Any fool who continues doing something long after it has ceased to be relevant or useful is said to be indefatigable.

Indefinite article | Article about global warming written by someone who enjoys foreign holidays.

Indenture | Where tomato seeds and grape pips invariably end up.

Independence | The demand of young people to be answerable to banks and credit card companies rather than their parents.

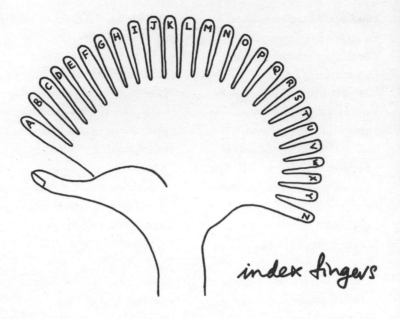

index fingers

Index finger | Archaic term. Now renamed the DVD remote-control finger.

Indirect taxation | Ingenious method of acquiring revenue from children, pensioners and invalids.

Industrial relations | Very heavy petting.

Industry | The past tense of heritage.

Ineffable | Unattractive, i.e. incapable of being effed.

Ineligibility | Occasion for sadness among DSS benefit staff.

Infallibility | Quality possessed by popes and A level students.

Infant | Child for whom Junior Calpol is already losing its kick.

Infanta | A cheap way of cooking duck a l'orange.

Inferiority complex | An arrangement of buildings devoted to British tennis coaching.

Infinitive | In grammar, a chance to wrongly go.

Inflation | Economic process which drives children's sweets to get smaller and smaller.

Influenza | Any cold in a man with a posh education.

Informal talks | Informal arguments.

Information | Facts which only the police still rely on the public to provide. Everyone else resorts to the internet.

Infrared | That part of the electromagnetic spectrum which controls garage doors.

Ingredient, vital | Any item absent from a supermarket's shelves. It is always on order. It is always expected in their next delivery. It is never known quite when that will be. It is never actually that vital.

Inherit the earth, the meek shall | But the not-so-meek shall charge them 40 per cent in tax.

Inhuman | Human.

Initial doubt | Sales assistants' concern over validity of customer's signature.

Injury time | The OAPs' name for winter.

Ink | The first fluid applied to newsprint. Cats supply the second.

Innocent 'til proven guilty | Highly suspicious 'til proven otherwise.

Inns of Court | Inn the news, Inn the dock, Inn the Masons, Inn the clear.

Innovations | Curious name for a catalogue always offering the same old crap.

Inscription | Proud moment for authors. They will gladly pen any words on a flyleaf happy in the knowledge that the book can then no longer be returned to its publishers.

Insert | Any irritating, unwanted literature placed inside magazines for the purposes of advertising – with the exception of the *Journal of the Royal College of Surgeons* where it has been simply left inside by mistake.

Insomnia | The result of worry over sleeping-pill side effects.

Instant access | The primary benefit of under-bed banking.

Instruction, religious | 1. Buy rucksack. 2. Insert bomb. 3. Record farewell video.

Instructions | Technical guide printed in a plethora of languages so people of all nations can disregard them equally.

Insurance | A tax on fear.

Integral to the plot | 1. Any nude scene in an 'art' film. 2. Every nude scene in a porn film.

Intellectual | Any person who admires Lord Bragg as much for his mind as the fact he still has a full head of hair.

Intellectual property | Houses in Hampstead, Tuscany and Hay-on-Wye.

Intensive care | Private health care.

Internet | A terminal disease – especially for record shops, public libraries, private libraries and the art of letter-writing.

Interval | Concession made by modern playwrights to audience enjoyment.

In-tray | Any tray favoured briefly by much-photographed celebrities. It becomes an 'out-tray' the moment a cheaper lookalike is made available to the masses in high street stores.

Inventory | List of things yet to be broken.

Investigative | Euphemism for rude or nosy. Thus, a peeping Tom would be described as an investigative pervert.

Invisible man | Man on bicycle in heavy traffic.

IOU | Three little letters that can mean so much.

Ironic | Any crass statement which causes offence is claimed afterwards to have been ironic.

Isobar | Line connecting areas of equal viewer confusion on hi-tech TV weather maps.

Isolation unit | The iPod.

Italian parliament | Roman political drop-in centre.

J | A type of special blue cloth so revered by student flat-sharers that they actively shun getting it wet or dirty.

Jack of all trades | Now losing work to the Polish Jan of all trades.

Jack Spratt | Early cholesterol scaremonger.

Jacket, sports | Jacket with paint or food company name emblazoned upon it.

jaardvark

Jade | Formerly a disreputable woman or a worn-out old nag. Now an ex-reality TV show contestant. Plus ça change.

Jail | Monopoly hazard, soon to be replaced by medical reports and community service.

Jam session | A lengthy meeting of the EU Conserves, Preserves and Pectin-related Foodstuffs Sub-Committee.

Jam, traffic | An encouraging sign of continuing consumer investment in the automobile trade.

Jaunt | Newspaper term. Any foreign trip made by a minister to a disaster-free location.

Jaunty angle | Angle invariably taken on last item on local TV news.

JCB | The digger de rigueur.

Jehovah's Witnesses | Religious zealots, called Witnesses because they wear suits, swear on the Bible, and will answer any stupid question put to them.

Jekyll | Doctor with evil *alter ego* more suited to work as his receptionist.

Jerry-built | A corruption of German-built, i.e. well made.

Jesus Christ | 1. Robert Powell. 2. An expression of mild annoyance. 3. Charismatic Hebrew freedom-fighter who, rising above the stigma of disputed parentage and the lower middle-class tradesmen mentality, led a campaign of peaceful non-cooperation against Palestine's Roman occupiers. Betrayed to authorities in a leadership power struggle and martyred after public show trial.

Jet propulsion | Means of achieving rapid acceleration – especially in carbon emission figures.

Jiffy bag | Envelope used to alert post office to damage opportunities.

'Jingle Bells' | Song celebrating the delights of seasonal joy-riding.

Jobs for life | Undertaker, gravedigger, etc.

Jocular | Of or pertaining to Scotland.

Jodhpurs | Trousers that go with a Jilly Cooper jacket.

John Bull | Personification of England with unfortunate bovine associations given BSE and foot and mouth.

Johnny come lately | Correct pronunciation of the name actually spelled Johnny Cholmondeley-Leatherstone-Lisle.

Joined-up government | Military rule.

Jojoba | Plant joos seeds just jappen to jelp your jair.

Journey, spiritual | The long trip necessary to find your nearest working church.

Joy-riding | A plea by youth for better public transport.

Judas | Early victim of freelancing pressures.

Judicious | Fragment of old washing-up advertising slogan, i.e. 'hands that judicious can be as soft as your face…' etc.

Juggernaut | A lorra lorra lorry.

Junta | *The South American Journal of New Military Writing.*

Jury, hung | Six of one, half a dozen of another.

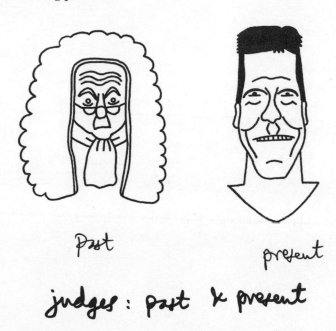

judges: past & present

K | 1. Salary unit. 2. Letter abused by morons in an attempt to make sad businesses sound fun, e.g. Kleen-a-Kar Ltd, Konkers NiteSpot, etc. See also Kwik.

Kabbalah | Kabbollochs.

Kaftan | Darkened complexion resulting from sitting too close to any greasy spoon's UV fly-killer.

Kangaroo | Animal with built-in 'Shopping Bag for Life'.

Kent, Clark | Journalist supposedly with super powers but yet to come up with lucrative Royal expose book.

Kentucky Fried Chicken | Rare example of a popular youth product being promoted by an aged, white-haired and bespectacled military figure.

Kept woman | The result of hormone-replacement therapy.

Kerb crawler | Errant motorist attempting to suck up to traffic warden.

Keyhole | A low-tech personal surveillance device.

Keyhole surgery | 'Small incision' technique invented by surgeons to reduce the likelihood of leaving the larger implements inside the patient.

Kid | Pejorative term hated by children who want to be thought of as adults without actually behaving like them.

Kidding, just | Kidding, only just.

Kidnapping | The holding of people against their will. Illegal everywhere except airport lounges, supermarket queues, French motorways, etc.

Killing time | The Glorious Twelfth.

Kindred spirits | Two or more people with the same line in bigotry.

King for a day | Now highly optimistic prediction about the length of Charles the Third's reign.

Kingdom, United | Kingdom when asked opinion of the French.

Kinky | Term used about any unusual sexual practice, e.g. chastity, fidelity, etc.

Kipper | Piscine victim of passive smoking.

Kit, Airfix | The future of British aeronautical construction.

KitKat | Two biscuit-fingers to dieting.

Kitsch | Rubbish enjoyed by intellectuals. Rubbish enjoyed by lesser mortals remains rubbish.

Kiwi | A Dralon-covered tasteless fruit.

Koi carp

not-so-koi carp

Knife, Swiss Army | Pocket knife, to be replaced by the Joint European Whittling Utensil if funds are available.

Knoll, grassy | Dallas recreational space, popular with invisible gunmen.

Knot, granny | Hitch used to restrain residents in old people's homes.

Koran | The best-selling prequel to *The Satanic Verses*.

Ku Klux Klan | The original Hoodies.

L | Plate inviting sympathy and consideration from other drivers towards a future fellow road fund and petrol duty payer.

Label-conscious | 1. Young people in Covent Garden. 2. Old people in botanic gardens.

Labour of love | Trying to find a petrol station still selling roses on 14th February.

Labour-saving device | 1. The coil. 2. A decade or more of economic stability.

Labyrinth | Tortuous path once leading to Minotaur; now ending in vacant post office counter window.

Lactation | Handy secondary use for breasts too small to sell newspapers.

Lactose | How to spot former polar explorers at the swimming baths.

Ladybird | Insect subject of socially conscious nursery rhyme condemning absentee parents with children at risk from fire-trap home. The children are 'gone' – having been taken into care by social workers.

Lady-in-waiting | Result of usual long queue for throne-room.

Lady-killer | Postcode prescribing.

Lager | The Bottle of Britain (ultimate victor: Germany).

Lambing time | Occasion for the overuse of sound effects in *The Archers*.

Lame duck | Waterbird with politicial ambitions.

Lamé duck | Waterbird with theatrical ambitions.

Lame excuse | Reason given for destroying racehorses.

Lancashire hotpot | Quality dope from the Bolton area.

Landfill | A mass grave for packaging.

Landlady | HM the Queen.

Landlord | The Duke of Westminster.

Lane, memory | Street still safe to wander down at night.

Language, foul | Footballing English – both on the pitch and on the terraces.

Languish | What Britons are said to do in foreign jails.

Lapse, memory | Condition affecting defendants.

Lark | Bird seen rarely by the unemployed.

Larva lamp | See Glowworm.

Laser | A dangerous weapon in the wrong hands, e.g. a businessman with a fully loaded flipchart and lots of little things he's keen to point out.

Last day! Everything must go! | Open again on Monday with the same stock.

Last word | See Zzzzzz.

Lateral thinking | 1. Standard student excuse for being still in bed at noon. 2. Thinking about sex. (See 1.)

largesse

Latter day saints | Bob Geldof, George Clooney.

Laughable | Said of anything not at all amusing.

Laughing gas | Vapour formerly used by dentists to mask pain. Now seemingly administered to TV sit-com audiences for much the same purpose.

Laughs last, he who | A TV critic, usually.

Lavatorial humour | Stand-up for men, presumably. Sit-down for women.

Lavish | Toilet-like.

Law-abiding citizen | Citizen lacking in opportunity for law-breaking.

Lawn | A decking opportunity.

Lead balloon | A poorly received idea, unlike the new eco-friendly unleaded balloon.

Leap in the dark | Primary flea attack strategy.

Learning curve | Not to be confused with an 'academic bent'. Learning curves are always 'steep'. In the private school sector this matches the fees that must be paid to achieve them.

Learning difficulties | Unruly classmates, lack of breakfast, over-testing, etc.

Least said, soonest mended | Guiding principle behind the average GP's three-minutes-per patient consultation.

Legal process, due | See Legal process, slow.

Leather, hell for | Saltwater, anything greasy, ice cream, etc.

Legendary | Any musician who has not worked for years is described as legendary.

Leg-warmers | 1. Over-long socks. 2. Over-familiar dogs.

Lemming | Creature whose behaviour is yet to be explained by exam stress, credit card debt, or mortgage worries.

Leonardo | A now distant historical figure – having been one of the Teenage Mutant Ninja Turtles.

Leopard | Endangered big cat getting harder and harder to spot.

Leotard | Origin of the phrase 'too close for comfort'.

Letter of the law | A summons.

Lettuce | The prawn-cocktail's winding sheet.

Level-pegging | Borderline autistic laundry.

Ley line | Mystical straight line passing through all the landmarks of importance to New Age followers: cyber cafés, charity shops, benefit offices, etc.

Liability | About the only thing most people won't accept nowadays.

Lib Dems | Party whose leaders over the last 30 years have included a man implicated in an attempted contract killing, an adulterer, an alcoholic and, most scandalously of all, a man over 60. Only the latter seems to have resigned without pressure. They remain mystified as to the reason for their long absence from power.

Lie detector | A soon-to-be unmarried woman.

Life and limb | Key Rottweiller objectives.

Life-long fan | Fan well-exceeding manufacturer's warranty period.

lichen   *dislichen*

Limerick | There once a five-lined verse, Whose form was a bit of a curse, By lines three or four, You've either heard it before, Or are just hoping it doesn't get worse.

Limited company | What so many businessmen prove to be.

Linen | Mystifying natural fibre which, when made into tea towels, is virtually indestructible yet when made into clothes has to be dry-cleaned only.

Lion | Once noble beast now reduced to making appearances on eggs and England sportswear.

Lip service | Once-yearly collagen implants.

Listed building | Building someone somewhere wants to pull down.

Lite | An Americanism. The 'lite' form of 'light'.

Literally | Synonymous with not at all, as in 'I was literally starving, literally broke', etc.

Literature | Word so abased it is now used to cover promotional leaflets for savings schemes, washing machines, etc. Much of it falls into the category of fiction.

past

present

looters: past & present

Liberty, Statue of | Curiously two-edged symbol of America for immigrants – a white woman in flowing robes bearing a flaming torch.

Licence to kill | 1. Driving licence. 2. Planning permission.

Liposuction | Costly technique allowing cosmetic surgeons to live off the fat off the land.

Litter | Trade term for loose magazine advertising inserts.

Livelihood | When threatened with its loss, any miserable job which the holder has hated all their life is said to be their livelihood.

Liver | Secretes bile when not doused in alcohol. See also Newspaper columnist.

Livestock | Stock yet to be suspected of Foot and Mouth.

Local anaesthetic | In Somerset, cider. In Scotland, whisky. In Buckfast, tonic wine, etc.

Logistics | Business term meaning yet more lorries on the road.

Look back in anger | The correct use of the mirror in motoring.

Loose-leaf notebook | Log kept by Network Rail of possible risks to autumn services on tree-lined tracks.

Lottery, National | An excuse to show yet more balls on TV on Saturdays.

Lout | French for the exit.

Love | Sex.

Love of money | The scenic route of all evil.

Lucky dip | Brief British seaside swim in which one manages to avoid any sanitary waste.

Lukewarm reception | The Australian response to British beer.

M | Summertime traffic-jam prefix.

Madcap scheme | Any attempt to appeal to kids by having a politician wear a baseball cap.

Madding crowd, far from the | Where someone is already planning to put a mobile phone mast or a windmill.

Made for each other | Phrase now true only of Frankenstein's monster and his bride.

Made to measure | Estate agents, HIPs assessors and insecure young men and women.

Mafia, the | Sinister Sicilian organisation who seem to control everything in

past   present

madonna & child: past & present

America bar their depiction in TV and films.

Magnesia, Milk of | Stomach medicine provoking confusion in the lactose-intolerant indigestion sufferer.

Magnet for thieves | 1. Broadcasting cliché for any event or situation that attracts criminals. 2. Top-selling gadget in the 'Crimmovations' catalogue. It fits through most household letterboxes, extends up to 15 feet, and will lift up to 400 grammes of keys.

Magnificat | A premium brand of cat food.

Magnolia | A subtle blend of white paint and dirt.

Magpie | Bird with criminal tendencies. See also Hooded crow, Heroin gull, Chavfinch, and ASBOcet.

Mainline | 1. Railway track. 2. To inject a drug less frequently on Sundays and bank holidays due to engineering works.

Maintenance man | A divorcee.

Maize | DIY cornflakes.

Majority voting | Historic British voting system in which the majority don't actually vote and the largest minority actually wins.

Make something of it?, Wanna | Belligerent approach to classroom craft activities.

Make-up | Facial cosmetics whose appeal to cabin crew and perfume counter girls alike never wears thin.

Malcontent | Person earning less money than his neighbour.

Male chauvinist | Man who puts women on a pedestal – along with a pole and baby oil.

Malice aforethought | Government long-term policy.

Mall | A place where tacky, over-priced goods are sold, leading down to Buckingham Palace.

Mallard | Fan of dull shopping centres.

Mammal | Creature capable of both suckling young and adding tap water to milk powder.

Mammoth task | Stopping the wild elephant going the same way.

Management, middle | Executive diet plan.

Manboob | Rare bosom where men are keen on a lack of size.

Mandrill | Check fly before appearing in public.

Manger, away in a | Franglais for 'Gone to lunch'.

Manhole | Aperture reluctantly exposed to medical practitioners unless travelling on the same rugby club coach.

Mania | Press cliché for mild public interest they wish to whip up into something much larger.

Manicurist | A hand job.

Man in the street | 1. Average person in Britain. 2. Suspicious character in gated estate in America.

Manmade fibre | Bran Flakes.

man friday   man, friday

man fridays: past & present

Man of the cloth | 1. Waiter. 2. Snooker player.

Man of the woods, old | 1. Rural victim of 'care in the community'. 2. A flasher.

Man or a mouse? Are you a | Sceptical child's question to rodent-costumed actor at Disneyland, Paris.

Mandate to govern | Voted into office by less than half of the population.

Mangle | Item of post office machinery.

Manual labour | 1. The effort required to lift most computing instruction books. 2. Consequence of refusing Caesarian.

Map | Mythical pre-sat nav chart of ancient knowledge, capable of being read by just a few wise men.

Marijuana | Apparently no worse for you than the average Home Secretary.

Mark of a man, the | Seat splash.

Marquis de Sade | French noble keen on inflicting pain, primarily through several execrable novels.

Marriage | Former tax loophole, now closed.

Marriage of convenience | Relationship heading into the toilet.

Mars | The god of chocolate.

Marvel of the age | Some new-fangled wonder.

Marvel of the aged | Some old-fangled wonder, such as Tony Benn, John Mortimer, Oliver Postgate, etc.

Marxists | 1. Groucho. 2. Harpo. 3. Chico. 4. Pinko.

Mask, face | Item worn by surgeons to reduce chance of positive identification in event of negligence charges.

Masochism | A morbid desire to travel by coach.

Masturbation | Digital sex.

Matt finish | Perpetual fear of the *Daily Telegraph* editor.

Maybe | The politically deferred no.

Meal, square | TV dinner eaten during *EastEnders*.

Mealtime | Down to as little as 40 seconds for some schoolkids and overstressed office workers.

Measure of success | Now clearly seems to be the metre.

Meat | Animal protein that vegetarians buy from

supermarkets in metal tins or plastic pouches to feed to their non-native, introduced, semi-captive pets because 'It's only natural'.

Meat and two veg | A burger and two packs of fries.

Medal | Notorious example of a noun which is increasingly being used as a verb as in 'Did you medal?', i.e. 'Did you *win* a medal?' Nobly, British athletes are trying hard to halt its spread by holding back in major sports events.

Megabucks | 1. Coffee chain's super-sized outlet. 2. Their annual turnover.

Melting pot | Instant noodle-snack container after addition of boiling water.

Memo | Term used to dignify any petty complaint sent around an office.

Memory for faces, good | Useful gift for members of Michael Jackson's family to possess.

Menace, Dennis the | Proof that the *Beano* is a comic and not a journal of record. It depicts a juvenile delinquent with an unleashed dangerous dog yet his parents are married, his father works, his mum is a housewife, he doesn't skip school, and he prefers knitwear to sports clothing. Crazy!

Mental patient | In-patient unconcerned about MRSA

MEP | A Brussels spout.

Merchant of Venice | Trader constantly advertising a 'sale due to flood damage'.

Meretricious | And a happy New Year!

Merlin | Arthurian magician who ended life trapped inside a tree. May explain Paul Daniels's fear of bonsai.

Message, on | Sending a text. Compare to: 'Off message' – in a tunnel.

Messy divorce | 1. Any divorce where the husband is left in charge of the home. 2. Every divorce involving children.

Met. Office | Only office where staff are actively encouraged to sit and talk about the weather.

Metal detector | Device sensitive to extended guitar solos and head-banging.

Methane | Gas produced copiously by cows in their insane war against the climate.

Metrication | Process by which inches became centimetres, miles became kilometres, and people over 40 became nostalgia bores.

Metropolitan Police Force | Abbreviated to the Met to give more members a chance of spelling it correctly.

Miasma | Good reason for not buying a cat.

Microscope | A credit agreement reading aid.

Microwave | Oven invented just to prove that pub food *could* get worse.

Midas touch | See Golden handshake.

Midriff | How the remaining members of Status Quo presumably hope to die.

Midsummer Night's Dream | Plays under the name *Donkey Love* in Scandinavia.

Miles better | British attitude to kilometres.

Military cross | Tour of duty extended again, boots no good, etc.

Military intelligence | Well-known contradiction in terms.

Milk float | Result of cow grazing on flood plain.

Millennium | Period of 1000 years – the time it takes for most people to learn to spell the word correctly.

Milton Keynes | A university town happily free of students.

Mime | Form of drama which creates feelings of anguish in spectators which just cannot be put into words.

Minder | A large, aggressive heavy thoughtfully provided to prevent decent, honest people from accidentally coming into contact with pop stars and celebrities.

Mind set | The full two matching hemispheres of the brain. (So far, available only in grey.)

Minefield, legal | Minefield complying with UN statutes.

Minestrone | Child's strength Maxestrone.

Mineral rights | Inalienable right of young to drink Coca-Cola and Pepsi.

Mini bar | 1. Small fridge used to keep peanuts cold in hotel rooms. 2. Device producing incessant hum designed to drive hotel occupants to drink.

Minimalism | Concept of living advocated for others by burglars.

Minor transgression | A major mistake for people who work with children.

miscellaneous sales

Minotaur | Monster with the body of a man and the head of a bull. See also Hangover.

Mint | The last remaining Western monopoly: the flavour of toothpastes.

Miss United Kingdom | What US tourists do at the merest whiff of terrorism.

Mitre | Hat that must be worn by bishops when operating machinery or handling food.

Mixed marriage | Marriage between someone who's pregnant and someone who isn't.

Moaning Minnie | Disneyland 'cast member' annoyed by working conditions.

Mobile home | House built over old mine workings.

Mockery | Rest home for clapped-out satirists.

Mod cons | Case sensitive entry. See also MOD cons: 'Home by Christmas', 'Peace-keeping operation', 'Full military pension', etc.

Moderate | Description of any right-winger in favour of hanging, but vehemently opposed to drawing and quartering.

Moment in time, at this | The windbag's 'now'.

Momma, red hot | See Hormone replacement therapy.

Monastery | Belgian lager factory.

Monopoly | About the only contest an old boot still stands a chance of winning.

Moon, cow that jumped over the | Cow suspected of steroid abuse.

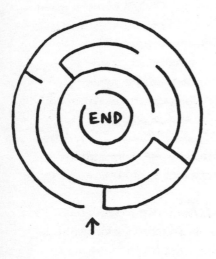

moral maze

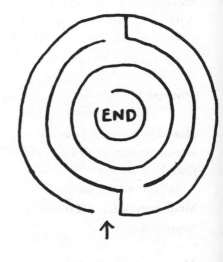

immoral maze

past

present

morning stars : past & present

Morse code | Now obsolete. A dashed shame.

Motherhood | A career hazard.

Motivation | Money.

Motive | What the police attempt to find after failing to find the criminal.

Moules marinierc | French for 'seaside donkeys'.

Mousetrap, the | Long-running play that if it contained swearing, sex and 'difficult themes' would have been loved by the critics and closed after two weeks.

Mouth-to-mouth | A survival technique, particularly for cold-sore viruses.

Moves in mysterious ways | 1. God. 2. Rowan Atkinson.

Mugshot | Tony Blair's preferred 'tea-drinking' photo opportunity.

Music to one's ears | See iPod.

hawk moth

kate moth

moths

Muslim | Suspicion now held about anyone with a beard, male or female.

MySpace | Social networking site oddly popular with claustrophobics.

Mystery tour | Rural taxi ride with driver who can't yet afford sat nav.

Mysticism | An alternative explanation of life and the universe made by people still annoyed that they couldn't understand physics at school. As a result they all claim that 'Science has failed us.'

Naff | Term used to judge something as outmoded or hackneyed, e.g. the continued use of the word 'naff' itself.

Naïve | To receive your FREE definition of this word send an SAE to the address at the front of the book, enclosing a £5.50 handling charge.

Naked ambition | To one day pose for Spencer Tunick.

Naked eye | The full extent of public female nudity in Saudi Arabia.

Nanny state | Gran Canaria.

Narrow-minded | Anorexic.

National Anthem | 'Here we go, here we go, here we go ...'

National Curriculum | Attempt to standardise UK teaching so that children end up being able to spell words like 'curriculum'.

National Grid | Formerly crosswords, now sudoku.

National Park | 1. Alton Towers. 2. Wembley.

past

present

navel oranges:
past & present

Nationwide | Any event that doesn't just happen in London.

Nature, Mother | A battered wife.

Nature-lover | 1. Briton with well-stocked garden bird-table and three pet cats. 2. Briton who worries about African rhinos and Amazon forests but would be hard-pushed to identify an elm or a reed warbler or a slow–worm, etc. 3. Claim always made by anyone who hunts.

Naturist holiday | Holiday where loss of luggage by airline presents no great problems.

Nearest and dearest | Key shopaholic strategy when pressed for time.

Necessary force | Level of force unnecessary before things were allowed to get out of hand.

Neckline | Confidential 24 hours telephone counselling service for concerned or distressed giraffes.

Needless to say | Verbal cliché used to make a superfluous statement even longer.

Negative equity | The union for really bad actors.

Neighbourhood Watch | See Peeping Tom. (Then ring the police.)

Neither fish nor foul | Vegan dietary credo.

Neon | A noble gas – except when used in lurid illuminated signs.

Neptune | 1. Powerful Roman god of the underwater world. 2. A seafood pizza.

Net profit | Money made from selling junk on eBay.

Neutral | Any country with too small an army to stand a chance of winning battles declares itself neutral.

Neutron bomb | Atomic device whose radiation blast is meant to leave property in the vicinity undamaged. Ironically, however, it will at the same time kill all estate agents.

New! Improved | Tacit admission by manufacturers that old product could have been better designed.

New man | One who has read enough babycare books to really annoy women by telling them what they are doing wrong.

New moon | Interesting use of the word 'new' in a sense shared by both marketing and astronomy. It is of course just the same old moon presented in a different light.

Newsflash | Any celebrity wardrobe malfunction.

Newt | Blameless creature unfairly associated with excessive drinking. It is only ever legless when a tadpole, and being amphibious, it spends most of the year dry.

New Year's Day | Classic hangover time – the morning after the year before.

Niche-marketing | The sale of things people don't want to the precise small group of people who don't want them the least.

Nicotine patch | Small plot where tobacco plants are still grown.

Nightclub | Desperate attempt to make the Royal Astronomical Society sound trendy.

past

present

nosebags: past & present

Nightmare, your worst | A local planner's dream come true.

Nipple count | Scheme to encouragenumeracy among *Daily Sport* readers.

No longer with us | 1. Dead. 2. Listening to iPod.

No through road | An open challenge to all 4X4 drivers.

Nocturnal e-mission | Late night internet searches, often for dubious websites.

Nodding dog | Dog responding to question about the need for more trees in cities.

No-go area | Bad news for Japanese board game fans.

Non-alcoholic | Warning placed on bottled waters.

Non-allergenic | Bizarre boast made by certain skin creams as if it was more than you might expect for them not to give you a rash.

Nonsense, utter | What government spokesmen do.

Non-sequitur | Advanced aardvark pastry-making.

Non-stop entertainment | What neighbours enjoy loudly.

Non-violence | Principle uniting Quakerism and American professional wrestling.

Northern lights | The Blackpool illuminations.

Nose dive | Budget rhinoplasty premises.

Nose, pay through the | The high cost of cocaine abuse.

Nose up, turn one's | Instruction to cosmetic surgeon.

Nostril | Cocaine and/or finger receptacle.

Novel idea | An old idea written with more sex in it this time.

Novelty value | Always far less than what you paid for it.

Number of the beast | Now changed to 0208 666.

Nutrient | Chemical added to breakfast cereal to allow it to be sold as a food.

nubile phone

O | How Britons over 40 still spell GCSE.

Oak, royal | Tree able to converse on equal terms with Prince Charles.

Oar | EU bureaucratic instrument.

Oats, getting one's | Sex. (Warning: may cause chaffing.)

Obesity epidemic | Public health theory rapidly gaining weight.

Obituary | In broadsheet newspapers, the last you'll ever hear about someone you'd never heard about before. In tabloids, a fresh chance to run all the old embarrassing photos of a celebrity.

Obligation, moral | No obligation whatsoever.

Obliging, very | Shop assistant working on commission.

Obscene publications | *Guns 'n' ammo, Soldier of Fortune, New Survivalist,* etc.

Observance, Lord's Day | Watching TV on Sunday.

octopus   octoplus

Obsolete | Any still perfectly good device for a which a more expensive and temperamental replacement has been developed.

Obstacle course | Particularly taxing stretch of pavement for both those with pushchairs and cyclists.

Occasional table | The dining table – given the trend for eating in front of the telly.

Occupation, reserved | Restaurant critic.

Occupied territory | In Britain, a public toilet cubicle. In Palestine, a PR debacle.

Octet | String quartet with job-sharing imposed.

Octopus | Rare creature capable of texting, changing a CD, eating pizza and driving safely all at the same time.

Ouevre | French vacuum cleaner.

Offerings, burnt | Barbecued party food.

Off-hand remark | Judge's Islamic law ruling on punishment for convicted thief.

Official | Synonym of dull, as in official biography, official history, official business, etc.

Off message | An abusive text.

Off-the-wall | How thieves will have your hanging baskets.

Oh dear | Phrase which police are specially trained to deliver sarcastically.

Old country, the | Eastbourne and its environs.

Oil | Lubricant, such as olive oil or whale oil, generally named after its source, though thankfully this no longer applies to baby oil.

Olive branch | Sole remains of olive grove after heavy shelling from opposite hillside.

Olympic ideal | Undetectable steroids.

Omission, sin of | Leaving a sportsman out of a side.

Omnipresent | 1. God. 2. CCTV. 3. Muzak.

Omnivorous | Eats both the burger and the chips.

On and off | When – and how – couples with small children get to make love.

One man band | The Corrs.

Online | Bad news for: 1. Salmon; 2. Family of compulsive gambler.

Onus | An insufficient bonus.

Open all hours | What shops now are, and churches are no longer.

Open verdict | A lack of judgement.

Opinion, public | Some pollster's opinion of your opinion.

Opposition, Her Majesty's | Prince Charles.

Optimist | Person not up to date with the news.

Oral history | *The Toothbrush: Its Pivotal Role in Public Health from 1700 to the Present Day.* Forward by Janet Street Porter.

Ordeal | Sane person's view of *Deal or No Deal.*

Ordnance Survey Map | Farmers' guide to footpaths due for ploughing.

owl

jowl

Orgasm | The end to months of speculation for Mrs Sting.

Ornithology | Branch of zoology by which rare and migrant birds get to catch a glimpse of Bill Oddie.

Orthodox church | Most churches built before about 1950 – after which they started to look a bit silly.

Orthopaedic mattress | Excuse given by hotel management for any uncomfortable bed.

Outdoors, the great | Smoker's view of the countryside.

Out-of-body experience | Vomiting.

Outwit | Stephen Fry, Graham Norton, Sandi Toksvig, etc.

Ovenproof | Crockery that only the dishwasher alone can ruin.

Overnight success | Any artist or performer ignored for years by critics and then chosen at random to be praised. After twelve months he is declared a 'spent force' and allowed to quietly continue his career. After twenty years of obscurity he is then 'rediscovered' and hailed a 'forgotten genius'. He then dies and is described in obituaries as a 'sad recluse'.

Overpowering scent | The smell of money.

Oxymoron | See Blindness.

Oyster | Mollusc emblematic of humorous lexicographers – an acquired taste, often hard to get into, and even harder to swallow, but where in some instances prior irritation produces pearls.

Ozone | Gas destroyed by deodorant manufacturers to the benefit of sun block producers.

P | 1. A car park. 2. Unit of money for car park.

Pacemaker | Unusual device that actually comes with batteries included.

Pacificist | Former believer in WMDs.

Pacifist, extreme | Pacifist lobbying for a change of name to pacihand.

Pack of lies | Collective noun for journalists.

Package holiday | 1. The mystery tour taken by second-class parcels before their eventual delivery. 2. Foreign trip for purposes of drug-smuggling.

Pad, A4 | The largest size of apartment still affordable in Knightsbridge.

Pages from history | Out-of-date web content.

Painkiller | Death, being cheap, free from side effects, and readily available on the NHS.

Palindrome | Michael Palin's personal airfield to accommodate his many trips abroad.

Palette | A minor friend.

Palisade | 1. Sparkling corgi juice. 2. Concert for impecunious royalty.

Palmed off | See Masturbation.

Palm Sunday | Church service offering free Holy Land style bookmark for every attendee.

Panda car | Car owned by driver with just a black and white licence.

P & P | Outcome of excess tea-drinking.

Panic | State of affairs in which the true British character is revealed: we rush out to queue for things – petrol, diesel, inoculations, etc.

Panic room | The kitchen on Christmas Day.

Panic stations | Any Tube stop where somebody thinks they can smell smoke.

Pantomime | Seasonal winter-time farce involving dames, barons, royalty and various rogues and villains. Not to be confused with the New Year's Honours List.

Pants | Word now meaning 'poor quality', and continuing a noble British tradition of underwear-related euphemisms. For example, a criticism of barristers' mistakes might be phrased: 'Knickers to pants briefs' bloomers.'

Papal Bull | Bull with dim view of artificial insemination.

Paperboy | A bringer of bad news.

Par for the course | Any result or service worse than expected is said in this country to be par for the course.

Paradox | An undefinable quality.

Paranoia | The morbid suspicion that your psychiatrist secretly thinks there is nothing wrong with you.

Paramilitary | Any ad hoc army where the members have to provide their own uniforms and weapons.

Parapet | Unauthorised gundog.

Paraphrase | Media pundits' term meaning to remember incorrectly and then misquote badly the words of people much wittier than oneself, e.g. 'To paraphrase H. L. Mencken ...' etc.

I must pay attention in maths.
I must pay attention in maths.
I must pay attention in maths.
I must pay attention in maths.

parallel lines

Par avion | French for 'air mail'. Waterborne mail is labelled 'Par Evian'.

Parity | Pirates' birthday celebration.

Parkin | A piece of cake for northern Smart car owners.

Parking meter | Useful device installed to collect the revenue needed to pay the traffic warden needed to inspect the meters once installed.

Parquet | French chat-show host.

Part-exchange | See Organ-swap.

Partners | A non-married couple.

Partners, sexual | A very much non-married couple.

Part-time worker | Full-time worker with a smoking habit, a Facebook page and ebay account.

Partwork | Series of expensive magazines that builds week by week into a comprehensive, beautifully illustrated boot sale item.

Passenger | 1. A mobile phone operative. 2. Any person forced to sleep overnight in an airport terminal.

Passive smoking | Habit that now, thanks to legislation, people have to actively pursue.

Password | Computer security system that not only protects information but also encourages your children to become more observant.

Pastime, national |
1. Watching television.
2. Complaining there's nothing on.

Paternity suit | Dark suit worn by defendant to impress judges at child support hearing.

Patience | Available by keying ***99*** on most voicemail systems. Then press *33 and hold until answered.

Patient confidentiality | Excuse used by doctors for concealing errors.

Patio | A burnt-sausage holding area.

Patriot | Any foreigner in a country with a climate they don't like.

Patronising | (Don't worry about this one, it's not important.)

Pause for thought | To temporarily halt a DVD while deciding what next to eat.

Pavement | 1. A cycleway.
2. A canine lavatory.
3. Continuous linear display space for household waste come recycling day.

Pay-back time | Graduation day.

Pay day | A High Court ruling.

Pay per view | Purchasing principle applying to:
1. Satellite television; 2. Seaside postcards.

PC, Non- | Any Police Community Support Officer.

Peace dividend | Dividend of little interest to arms company shareholders.

Peacemaker | A blessed nuisance.

Peace pipe | A silent exhaust.

Peak rate | A phone call made from work.

Pear | Fruit yet to be described as typically 'woman-shaped'.

Pearly King and Queen | About the only British royalty for whom respect still remains.

Peat Moss | Kate Doherty's former partner.

Peaty | Whisky-maker's euphemism for foul-tasting.

Pecorino | Italian brand of Viagra.

Pedant | Person for whom little things really do mean a lot.

Pedestrian | A motorist unable to park immediately outside his house.

Peking duck | Wildfowl whose outspoken calls for democracy has seen it killed, roasted and hung in a window as a warning to others.

Pen | Now spelled PIN.

Penalty | Like the Great Barrier Reef, a spot popular with divers.

Pentagon | Building supporting the US military theory that there are five sides to every argument.

People who need people | 1. McDonald's. 2. Those involved in chain-letter profiteering scams.

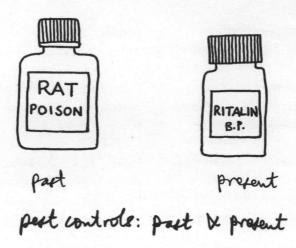

past   *present*

pest controls: past & present

People who knead people | Masseurs.

Pep talk | Financial advisory flim-flam.

Perfectly awful | The most common form of perfection.

Periodic table | Chart of vital importance to: 1. Chemists; 2. Would-be parents.

Perks | 1. Those items small enough to be stolen from work without detection. 2. Affectionate nickname for BBC radio's Brian Perkins.

Perm | Short for 'permanent' – hairstyle replaced every few weeks.

Peroxide blonde | Woman with a dark past.

Persecution complex | Guantanamo Bay.

Persistent vegetative state | A Southern state, presumably.

Persona non grata | Someone who doesn't like parmesan.

Personal assistant | Viagra.

Personal column | See above.

Personal identification number | The Beast, 0666. Roadies 1212. Tom Robinson 2468. Seb Coe 2012, etc.

Pessimist | Optimist who learns from experience.

Pet hate | Any dislike that has to be left with relatives during family holidays.

Petrol station | Curious use of the word station for a place where people set off on time and within budget and in relative comfort.

Pettifog | French mist.

Pew, take a | Antique thieves response to finding church unlocked.

Phallic symbol | Symbol still oddly absent from the standard computer keyboard.

Photocopy | The easiest way of making money.

Piano-tuner | Man sent to sabotage Harrison Birtwistle concert.

phantom pregnancy

Pick your brains | Fingernails in urgent need of trimming.

Pickpocket | Worker happy with the notion of a dip in wages.

Picnic, no | Any picnic with wasps.

Picture of health | See CAT scan.

Pie chart | Football ground catering league table.

Piercing scream | Shock at first encountering teenaged daughter's belly bar.

Pigeonhole | A place where crap: 1. Builds up; 2. Freely exits.

Pigheaded | 1. Child that will only eat sausage. 2. Medical science gone too far.

Pigmy | Economy-class passenger with sufficient legroom.

Pill, the | Great way of teaching teenage girls the days of the week.

Pillow fight | The struggle to get cheap hotels to give you an extra head rest.

Pimp | The other sort of solicitor a prostitute may have to pay.

PINs and needles | Using stolen credit cards to fund a drugs habit.

Pint-sized | Small. (See Brewer's droop.)

Piste | 1. A slope prepared for skiing. 2. A nervous Briton prepared for skiing.

Pitter-patter | Mobile kebab stand sales pitch.

Pitch black | Floodlights fused.

Pizza | Paradoxical fast food – a circular square meal.

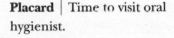

plain sailing   fancy sailing

Placard | Time to visit oral hygienist.

Placebo | Medicine that does nothing but still costs over six quid on prescription.

Plague on both your houses | Council tax.

Plaid | Patterned cloth worn in Scotland by Americans and in London by the Japanese.

Plankton, save the | Little-known Japanese pro-whaling pressure group.

Plaque, Blue | Circular tablet marking the former residence of some deceased famous person who, ironically, when alive was probably sick of people gawping at their property.

Plate, want everything on a | Over-demanding person, especially in a burger joint.

Playing field, level | Sportsground all ready for sale to developers.

Play, miracle | Any non-musical that stays open in the

West End for longer than three months.

Plot | 1. A piece of countryside. 2. The ever-present conspiracy to put houses on it.

Plot, essential to the | Hollow excuse made for clothed scenes in pornographic movies.

Plumber, 24-hour | Emergency plumber who takes a day to turn up.

Poacher turned gamekeeper | Poacher clearly given job without adequate Criminal Records check.

Point-blank | Clean driving licence.

Pointless | Any pencil within arm's length of a telephone.

Poker | Game of chance in which players have to bluff convincingly – especially when their partners ask if they've been playing it online all night.

Polar bear | Arctic animal whose survival is threatened by climate change, prompting thousands of people to fly to see them while they can.

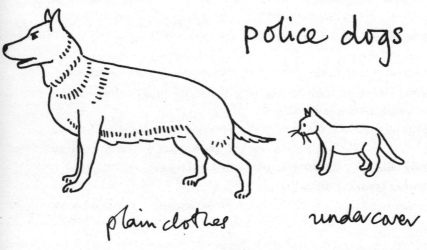

police dogs

plain clothes   undercover

Polecat | A cheaper and more reliable cat than the standard British moggy.

Police dog | Dog that not only sniffs arseholes but catches them too.

Police state | Ignorance.

Policy, not our | Mantra chanted by shop assistants faced with customers seeking a refund.

Political animal | Rat, toad, snake, ass, worm, louse, etc.

Political correctness | Calling a spade an alternatively morphic fork.

Political correctness gone mad | Offensive term for 'political correctness with an alternative view of reality'.

Pony tail | Dated male hairstyle inviting comparison of the wearer to a horse's rear.

Pool, indoor | Pet in need of house-training.

Popcorn | Last area of movie business where good taste is still a concern.

Porn | Material that excites: 1. Perverts; 2. Puritans.

Portable | Any impractically large or heavy object made with a small handle attached is sold as being fully portable.

Portion, individual | Intriguing use of the word 'individual' as a synonym for 'small'.

Posh | 1. Port Out, Starboard Home. 2. Parents own Stately Home.

Possession | Nine-tenths of: 1. The law; 2. *The Exorcist*.

Postgraduate | A PhD student (prolonging his/her debt).

Post haste | The rush to ruin Royal Mail.

Post-mortem | Likely outcome of above.

Post-natal depression | Result of having: 1. Babies; 2. Teenagers; 3. Elderly parents.

Potential to extend | Estate agent euphemism for 'You'll need to extend.'

Pot-holing | Inner-city cycling.

Prayer | Now renamed a P-mail. Sadly God gets a lot of spam.

Precocity | Any talent shown by other people's children.

Predisposed | How junk mail ideally should arrive.

Preferential treatment | Equal treatment of one's enemies.

Pre-marital sex | Now compulsory test of future physical compatibility. However, results can be inconclusive, and the test may need repeating for many years before a couple finally recognise they are incompatible, and the man marries someone younger.

Preparatory school | School that helps prepare parents for the cost of boarding school.

Preserved, well | Compliment paid to: 1. The long-lived; 2. The long dead.

Pretty as a picture | Euphemism nowadays for bloody ugly.

Price of fame, the | Phrase used by rich celebrities for no longer being able to shop unbothered in Woolworth's like all the lucky poor people.

prefix

postfix

Priceless | Supermarket item bearing barcode only.

Price tag | German shopping day.

Prince of Wales | For the anti-Camilla contingent, the heir abhorrent.

Prison | Place where criminals learn the error of their ways – from other criminals more skilled in housebreaking, stealing cars, etc.

Private income | Prostitution.

Probability theory | Principle behind the idea that an infinite number of monkeys sat behind an infinite number of typewriters for an infinite amount of time would eventually be a huge hit on reality TV.

Procrastination | See Elsewhere.

Procreation | What an alarming number of US science teachers are.

Prods, cattle | Arch-enemies of the Papal Bulls.

Product placement | Blatant practice common to films and television but shunned by *This Septic Isle* (Ebury Press).

Professional | Paid.

Professional, semi- | Paid by cheque.

Profit | The money raised by lowering standards.

Profit motif | The £ sign.

Profound | What actors think they are being when they regurgitate idiot clichés about life very slowly. Deeply profound actors also nod their heads in silence afterwards.

Pro-lifer | Person with strong anti-abortion stance, frequently resident in those American states operating the death penalty.

Prominent person | Socks in underpants suspected.

Promised land | What the Palestinians were.

Promoter, fight | Lager.

Property speculation The vague hopes of young people that they might one day be able to afford their own home.

Psychokinesis | How did this get here?

Protest, Peaceful | See Demonstration, noisy.

Proud father | Father just slightly taller than everyone else in the christening photos.

Prune | Plum resistant to the idea of Botox.

Psychedelia | Delia Smith's as yet unbroadcast mushroom cookery special.

Puberty | A hairy time for teenagers.

Public relations | Private affairs as reported in the press.

Publish and be damned | The late Aleister Crowley's modus operandi.

Pundit | Just what the author has done.

Pyramid selling | Major concern for the Office of Pharaoh Trading.

Q | 1. Much-missed Spike Milligan series. 2. The tasteless signwriters' 'queue'. 3. The third syllable of Bar-B-Q. 4. The second mysterious initial in 'B & Q'.

Quadrangle | Minor scuffle between rival academics.

Quadrant | Major argument preceding the above.

Quadraphonic sound | A useful attempt by hi-fi designers to allow music-lovers to authentically and expensively recreate in their own homes the effect of somehow having managed to slip unnoticed into the middle of a symphony orchestra or pop group while carrying an armchair.

Quadruped | Child under 18 months, adult over 18 pints.

Quail | To still be nervous about eating eggs.

Quakers | Spiritual movement with creed of respect, and non-violence, as exemplified by its most famous member, Richard Milhous Nixon.

Qualified | Weasel word used by con artists to blur the massive difference between theory and practice, e.g. 'I'll have you know, I'm a qualified palmist/reflexologist/iridologist/astrologer, etc.' Means little when the subject is hogwash to begin with.

Quality time | Greenwich Mean Time – the industry standard.

Qualms | Secret fears only ever revealed by smug bores after things have gone wrong.

Quarterstaff | Result of previous night's over-celebration at company Christmas party.

Queen bee | Bee that annoys all the other bees by continually asking them: 'And what do you do?'

Queen's English | Queen's actually part-German, part-Danish, part-Cockney, etc.

Question of sport | 'Ampoules, capsules or powder?'

Question mark | Bruise left on suspect during police interrogation.

Question time, Prime Minister's | Event curiously named as the Prime Minister gets to ask no questions.

Quick and the dead, the | The two categories of road-crossing pedestrians.

Quick-witted | Slow-witted *Have I Got News for You* panellist after crafty TV editing.

Quid pro quo | Latin for 'Cash on delivery'.

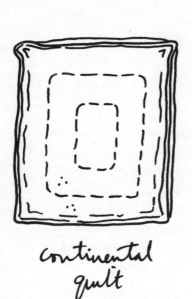

continental
quilt

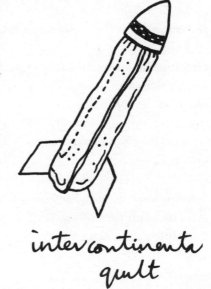

intercontinenta
quilt

quoit

quoitus

Quiet | What all murdering, psychopathic neighbours prove later to have been.

Quiet coach | The sort of personal trainer Davina McCall urgently needs.

Quiet life, anything for a | Enquiry made of pharmacist about range of tranquillisers available.

Quintessential | Word used to describe the only decent piece of work done by an artist in a long and otherwise undistinguished career. It

is said to be 'quintessential Smith', etc., despite the mountain of rubbish actually being more representative of his or her output.

Quirky | TV euphemism for any drama that was originally meant to be wildly amusing but instead just turned out to be irritating.

Quote | Amusing statement from either a literary personage or a builder. Even more entertainingly, neither will actually include VAT.

Rabies | Disease characterised by a fear of water and coincidentally known to be prevalent in France.

Race track | Any straight stretch of road free of traffic lights.

Racist | Any person who hates Robert Mugabe for the wrong reason.

Radiant | Tabloid description of any pregnant celebrity not actually pictured throwing up.

RADAR | Method most likely to be successful when trying to locate a staff member in the typical DIY warehouse.

Radiator | Domestic device for producing loud knocking sounds from lukewarm water.

Radicals, free | A danger to: 1. The immune system; 2. The Burmese system.

Rail | To complain loudly and angrily, hence the association with train travel.

Railcard | 'With deepest sympathy', 'Belated best wishes', etc.

Rainbow coalition | Alliance of aggrieved leprechauns concerned about financial security.

Rake, lawn | Weapon of Moss Destruction.

Rake's Progress, The | Hogarthian early example of the use of the term 'progress' to imply a decline in the quality of life.

Rank | 1. The provenance of most British films of the fifties. 2. The quality of most British films today.

Ransom note | A valiant attempt by the criminal fraternity to keep alive the art of letter-writing.

Ratbag | See Binbag.

Rattle, death | Painted baby toy with high lead content.

Razor, Occanis | The dictum that the simplest explanation of any given situation is of no interest to conspiracy theorists or students of the paranormal.

Reader, I married him | Proof, if it were needed, that *Jane Eyre* is a Victorian novel.

Reading room | Lavatory.

Reality TV | Artificially contrived TV.

Reaper, Grim | Agricultural worker with no worries about job security.

Recall, instant | Rare example of something instant being better than its more time-consuming alternative.

Reckoning, day of | 5th April, unless deferred due to appeal.

Recluse | Any celebrity who refuses to give press interviews.

Recognised authority | How the media describes any bore whose field is too dull or obscure for any other sane

ready cash

not ready cash

person to have bothered taking an interest in it.

Recommended retail price | A mythical exorbitant figure plucked out of the air by manufacturers to make the actual retail price of an article seem slightly less alarming by comparison.

Recorded delivery | The Queen's Christmas Day Speech. Even Her Majesty would rather not interrupt her lunch for that.

Red eye reduction | Drinking less cheap spirit.

Red-handed | Can't yet afford a dishwasher.

Reduced circumstances | Crcmstncs.

Refrigerator | Device for keeping salad vegetables chilled before throwing them away unused.

Refusenik | Council resident who will not co-operate with rubbish collection rules.

Rehabilitation | The process by which newly released convicts are once again made to feel part of society – the unemployed and homeless part.

Rehydration | All-pervading term for simply drinking a glass of water.

Reinforced concrete | Concrete with planning permission behind it.

Relative calm | Relative on Prozac.

Relief map | Gazetteer of massage parlours.

Religiously | Verb meaning to perform any task with a frequency reminiscent of devotion to sacred duty, i.e. every other Sunday or once a year at Christmas.

Remarkable likeness | Any effort by an official royal portrait-painter that is even half-recognisable as its subject.

Remedy | Word used for any alternative medicine or government measure that might not actually work.

Remembrance Sunday | Day on which *The Archers* is moved out of respect for the dead of two world wars.

Remind me again | Polite coded phrase meaning, 'I've completely forgotten what you told me as I wasn't really listening in the first place.'

Removal men | NHS dentists.

Rep. | Short for 'reprehensible', i.e. pertaining to salesmen.

Repetitive strain injury | Abbreviated to RSI to reduce the risk of the condition arising in those who have to type it out.

Replay, action | A rare treat for broadcasters: the opportunity to have a repeat of an original broadcast within that broadcast itself. Wow!

Representation | Name given to the defence of unemployed black teenagers by high-earning middle-aged white barristers.

Repressed | The button on every pelican crossing that doesn't respond immediately.

Reproduction | Furniture so poorly faked that it cannot be sold as the genuine article – even to Americans – is reluctantly admitted to be reproduction.

Reputation to consider, I have my | Line used by prostitute in rejecting a politician's custom.

Required reading | Very little nowadays, apart from medicine bottle instructions and credit agreement small print. Everything else is eventually adapted for television.

Research | Claim made by every actor caught in some criminal act.

Reserved | Every empty table in a restaurant where the waiters want to get home early.

Resign! | Dennis Skinner's cheery across-the-Commons greeting.

Resigning matter, not a | Any error by someone in public service short of infanticide; 24 hours later the claimant then resigns.

Respect | Now a synonym of fear.

Responsible adult | Man being hunted by child maintenance agency.

Restorer, picture | Satellite TV engineer.

Restrictive practice | Bondage session refresher.

Résumé | French term used by Americans for a Latin term (curriculum vitae) preferred by the British. Needless to say, the job will go to a Pole.

Retard | 1. A resurfaced road. 2. The person who schedules the works for 1. at a time of maximum traffic.

Retention, water | See Hosepipe ban.

Retro | Any horrid old clothes worn by young trendy people. Horrid old clothes worn by old non-trendy people are merely horrid.

Revenge | Great name for new ice cream dessert, being both sweet and best eaten cold.

Reversal of fortune | Enutrof.

Review copy | Any hardback on sale in a secondhand bookshop weeks ahead of the date it is due to be published.

Revised estimate | Building trade term. An increased estimate.

Revival, nineties | Not considered worth it in most NHS hospitals.

Revival, theatrical | The ham-acted on-field recovery of a footballer shamming a foul.

Revolutionary design | Use of the word 'revolutionary' as a synonym for 1. Uncomfortable. 2. Ugly.

Rhetoric, mere | Any eloquent, well-reasoned, impassioned speech made by an opponent.

Riddle of the sands | The allure of Clacton.

Ridicule | Embarrassing condition for which politicians appear to have found a vaccine.

Riding high | Jockey due to fail dope test.

Rife | 1. Drug-smuggling in Thailand. 2. The sentence if caught doing 1.

Rift valley | District of Los Angeles with high percentage of divorcees.

Right away! | Tomorrow.

Rights, human | Lager, Nike trainers and satellite TV.

Rigor mortis | God's way of telling us we should have relaxed more when we had the opportunity.

Ripe | Condition attained by most supermarket fruits about 2 or 3 weeks after the day of purchase. They then go rotten in an instant and have to be thrown away.

Risk, element of | Lead, radon, plutonium, etc.

Road sense |
1. Avoiding motorways.
2. Not owning a car.

Robbery, daylight | Result of turning clocks backwards in winter.

Rock bottom | 1. A low point. 2. Mr Jagger's rear. (See 1.)

Rocket science, it's not | See Botany.

Role model | Person set up as an example of how to behave well. (Cf. Parole model – an example of how to behave well for six weeks, then go back to being naughty.)

Roll-on, roll-off | 1. Modern ferries. 2. Modern sex.

Rolling Stones | Rare example of a group of old people for whom the young have respect and admiration.

Romance, holiday |
Brief affair lasting two weeks for most, six weeks for teachers.

Romantic movement | See Pelvic Thrust.

Room for improvement | Typically the loft, then the kitchen.

Rose-tinted spectacles | Glasses now shown to exacerbate short-sightedness, often with accompanying dewy-eyedness.

RoSPA | The Royal Society for the Prevention of Accidennts. Oh bugger…

Rostrum camera | Ken Morse.

Rotation, crop | The turning of market stall produce so that bad parts are hidden from customers.

Rotunda | What children are getting, seemingly by the day.

Rough and ready | The two prime qualities of Beaujolais nouveau.

Royal flush | Result of unexpected mention of Diana.

Rucksack | The burden of youth.

Rug-rats | 1. American slang for babies. 2. Major rodent pest worry for Elton John and others.

Rule of thumb | That the thumb shall appear in the foreground of all holiday photos.

Rustic charm | A horseshoe.

S

S | 1. Endangered dress size. 2. Any one of the three elements of a foreign beach holiday. 3. Any one of the two elements of a British beach holiday.

Sabotage | A public services cost-cutting measure.

Saccharin | Artificial sweetener used to allay the health fears of people who feel safer eating synthesised chemicals than they do eating sugar.

Sachet | French word used to give false dignity to irritating paper portions of artificial sweetener.

Sack race | The rush to get new work colleagues into bed.

Sacrifice, great | Those parents who forgo buying a Tuscan holiday home or a third car to pay the children's school fees are said – by themselves only – to have made a great sacrifice.

safe home

unsafe home

Sadness | Dire consequences of stopping anti-depressants.

Safe seat | 1. Commonly held view of any seat in a Tube carriage free from bearded passengers with luggage. 2. Incumbent MP's posterior in constituency with apathetic voters.

Safe sex | Chastity, as all other alternatives seem to involve some risk of pregnancy, infection, injury, RSI or choking.

Safety pin | PIN based on an obscure historical event that few others are likely to guess, e.g. the introduction of the cashpoint machine in 1967.

Sagomasochism | The enjoyment of school dinners.

Sailing, plain | Sails yet to suffer from the attentions of Cath Kidston.

Sake of the children, for the | 1. Reason given by ill-matched partners for continuing to stay together. 2. Reason given by ill-matched partners for choosing to separate.

Salad cream | Dismayonnaise.

Salary | 1. The money given to employees in return for work. 2. The greater amount given to company chairmen and directors in return for keeping down 1.

Sale of Goods Act | Extra dull act removed from final draft of Arthur Miller's *Death of a Salesman.*

Sales, January | Sales so-called because they begin on December 26th.

Sales resistance | 1. Poverty. 2. Death.

Salt, with a pinch of | How most dietary health scares should be taken.

Samaritans, the | About the only British organisation that doesn't cold call householders and hasn't yet had its operations moved to Bangalore.

Sample, free | The provision of urine, at no cost to the householder, by drunks who come into your garden at night.

Sandpaper | DIY essential graded, as for newspapers, according to their degree of coarseness.

Sanguine | French for 'penguin-less'.

Sanskrit | The language of the earliest Barbara Cartland novels.

Santa's little helper | Amphetamines.

Sarcasm | The lowest form of wit i.e. that used by policemen and magistrates.

Satisfactory condition | Curious phrase used by doctors to describe the state of any attack or accident victim who, despite horrific injuries, is now asleep in a hospital bed.

Sauce for the goose, sauce for the gander | Tomato ketchup, the universal condiment.

St George's Cross | Has just heard he is to be prosecuted for slaying endangered reptile.

St Swithin's Day | Typically the first day of the hosepipe banning season.

SAS | The military arm of the paperback industry.

Sash window | Staunchly Protestant glazing unit.

Saving | The extra money you haven't lost by buying something you don't need.

Savoury | Overall taste of any processed food where the salt and MSG content overpowers the added sweeteners.

Sawn-off shotgun | Only known method for getting money out of banks without having to provide excessive personal details and at a favourable rate of interest.

Scaffolding | Intricate metal bower erected by building workers for the purpose of sexual display.

Scaremonger | Shop keeper selling mobile phones, wi-fi connections, coffee, butter, red meat, alcohol, plastic toys from China, etc.

Scarecrow | Teenage fashion icon.

Scathing review | Journal rounding up the very best of contemporary scathing. Formerly *Scathes and Scathemen*.

Scatterbrain | Result of absentmindedly forgetting to put on seatbelt.

Scatter cushion | Self-serving description of any cushion a person cannot be bothered to replace on a sofa.

Scenery | Any range of hills visible from a road.

Sceptic | Person who believes all conspiracy theories are part of a global governmental plot to distract the masses from noticing what they're up to.

Schizophrenia | Mental illness in which the poor sufferer hears voices telling him he is too expensive to care for and would be better off walking the streets.

Scientist | Any person in a white coat who isn't selling meat, ice creams or make-up.

Scientist, mad | Scientist who thinks the general public have the faintest understanding of what he or she is up to.

Scissors | Dangerous cutting implement involved in fewer accidents nowadays thanks to children's growing inability to run.

Scoop | 1. A tabloid newspaper exclusive. 2. A device for picking up dog dirt.

Scorched earth policy | Banning disposable barbecues from parks.

Score, musical | One-nil, one-nil, one-niiiiiil, etc.

Scot-free | Unlikely description for any Labour cabinet.

Scottish National Party | Devolutionist group whose most famous supporter is Sean Connery – who lives in Spain.

Scout movement | Gentle edging away from over-friendly Scout master.

Scratch 'n' sniff | What hyperallergic people do all year round.

Screensaver | Any picture of a much-loved pet or family member that comes up on a computer when not being used to view pornography.

Scrotum | The only must-have bag for men.

Scurvy | Long time, no C.

Sealed, my lips are | Result of mistaking Prittstick for lipstick.

Sea level | One of the few standards expected to rise over the ensuing century.

Search engine | 1. Device which saves hours of your time trying to find things on the internet. 2. Device which wastes hours of your time by finding things on the internet.

Seasons, the | Nature's poor attempt to mimic the fashion industry. She remains, rather pathetically, up to six months behind.

Seaworthy | Judgement made of: 1. Ships; 2. Effluent.

Secondary sexual characteristics | Those that appear in secondary school.

Second fiddle | Y-fronts still maladjusted.

Sect | To be fired in South Africa.

Sectioned | 1. The insane. 2. Sunday newspapers.

Sedentary occupation | British workman's view of road-mending.

See-through | The principal appeal of: 1. The negligee; 2. The burka.

Self-educated | Pupil with unusually high regard for teacher.

Self-employed | Worker with unusually understanding boss.

Semi-conductor | Simn Ratl.

Seminal work | Bill Clinton's autobiography.

Semtex | Further proof that everything ends up made of plastic nowadays.

Senior moment |

Sentence, suspended | Death by hanging.

Sentry duty | Posing for photos next to US and Japanese tourists.

Sequel | Any American movie which is not a remake. There are no sequels to British films as the concept implies that some previous film made money.

Serious injury | The sort of injury which players of violent computer games find hilarious.

Serpent | Early salesman for Apple.

Seventy mph | A motorway speed limit. The upper limit is not specified.

Seven Wonders of the World | Wonder what's for tea? Wonder what they earn? Wonder what they look like naked? Wonder what they paid for that? Wonder if they're gay? Wonder if they're having an affair? Stevie Wonder.

Sexism | A gender agenda.

Sex object | A baby.

Shadow-puppet | Puppet insistent it could do a better job than the present incumbent puppet.

Shaken, badly | Any champagne bottle handed to some fool sportsman.

Shamrock | Any classic rock anthem rerecorded by the LSO.

Shape for your age, in good | Unsettling semi-compliment never used unless your age and shape are actually no longer what they used to be.

Shaver, electric | Ingenious device for removing all facial hairs but for one or two, which then grow to inordinate length.

She | 1. The cat's birth mother. 2. The cat's foster mother. 3. The cat's social worker. 4. The cat's parole officer. 5. The cat's brother (post-op, now wishes to be called Miss Frou Frou).

Sheaf | A cockney condom.

Shed | Unusually for the English language, a verb with two distinctly opposite meanings according to gender. 1. To jettison unwanted objects (female). 2. To hoard objects (male, derived from the name of the place where they end up).

Sheikh | Arabian aristocracy's gift to low comedy, as in Shiekhs Al-egg, N'Vac, Ratel En-rol, etc. See also Lords Elpus, Sprayer and Luffer-Ducke.

Shelter, bus | Simple roadside shelter erected to keep the rain off vandals while they get on with their work.

Shetland pony | Racetrack slang: £12.50.

Shit creek | A tributary of the Thames (paddling not advised).

Shoulderblade

single cream married cream sour cream

It won't last...

Shock absorber | Brandy, traditionally.

Shoehorn | See Foot-fetishism.

Shopper, mystery | That unknown person who must single-handedly be keeping our small high street shops afloat.

Short sight | Disability that is no bar to a job in government planning.

Shot in the dark | 1. Night-time drive-by murder. 2. Police guess as to who did it.

Shrine | Any historic national sporting venue.

Shut-down | Any down over which the army do manouvres.

Shuttle | 1. A bus. 2. A spaceship. Neither service is entirely reliable.

Sickbed | A fluton.

Signs of the times | '24 hrs CCTV surveillance', 'Guard dogs patrol these premises', 'No more than 2 schoolkids in shop at once, 'Red route', etc.

Silence | Increasingly scarce commodity. Used to be golden, now gone platinum.

Silk | Nature's poor attempt to mimic the harsh clammy lifelessness of nylon.

Similar | Not the same as 'the same as', but similar.

Similarity to any living person is coincidental | Principle underlying passport photos.

Simulator, flight | Small airless box in which one is confined with insufficient leg room while a tape plays of children screaming and a fat businessman snoring. On exiting, your luggage will be found to have been damaged or lost.

Sin | Increasingly popular place of residence.

Single market | Speed dating.

Sink, chained to the kitchen | What only the plug is nowadays.

Sirs | Common tabloid abbreviation for 'teachers' used in the same papers that

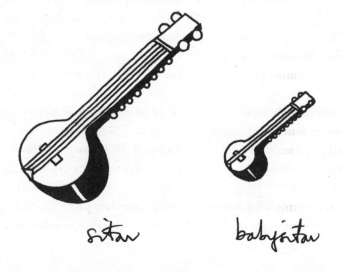

sitar   babysitar

typically bemoan declining standards of public literacy.

Skirl | Word specially invented to describe the peculiar horror of bagpipes.

Slapping, happy | What Grumpy was eventually prosecuted for.

Sleepy, you are feeling | Scurrilous accusation levelled at Snow White.

Sleeve | The modern built-in handkerchief.

Slice of life | Bread way past use-by date.

Slide rule | No adults. No stilettos. Socks must be worn.

Slug | Depressingly health-conscious creature – only eats salad and is paranoid about added salt.

Smart | Euphemism for stupid, as in smart weapon, smart drug, 'smart dress required', etc.

skategoat

Smells, bells and | 1. High Church practices. 2. Whisky-drinking vagrants.

Smile! | You're on CCTV!

Smile, and the world smiles with you | Now amended to 'Smile, and the world will think you're a bit odd in the head'.

Snail | Further proof that all things can be found in nature, including the caravan.

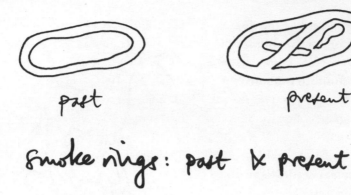

past

present

smoke rings: past & present

Snot | Substance like Al Gore. Green and gets up lots of people's noses.

Snowman, The | Raymond Briggs's frozen asset.

Social standing | Also known as queuing.

Society | Famously, according to Lady Thatcher, there was no such thing. Her ennoblement was therefore widely reported in the No Such Thing pages of the papers.

Soft | Word meaning 'not quite as bad as it could be', as in soft drugs, soft porn, soft sentence, soft furnishings, etc.

Soldier of fortune | Ex-soldier with lucrative publishing deal.

Solemn occasion | TV sitcom watching.

Soliloquy | Shakespearian forerunner of cabbies' conversation.

Solo | Opportunity created by jazz musicians for audiences to catch up on conversation.

Sorbet | 'Slush Puppy' for grown-ups.

Soul food | Chicken karma, beans on host, yom kipper, L Ron Rhubarb, etc.

Sparrow | Bird whose conviction for the murder of Cock Robin was largely based on confessional evidence.

Spate | The collective noun for burglaries.

Spectator sport | Modern view of street crime.

Speechless | Politician with autocue broken.

Spelling bee | Three-letter task which would tax quite a number of 11-year-olds.

Sphere of influence | Any ball in any ball game in a masculine environment.

Splinter group | The Carpenters.

Spoilsport | What Sky and ITV do with their excessive ad-breaks.

Sport of kings | Adultery.

Spot check | Dismal routine for teenagers.

Square-leg | 1. Cricket position. 2. Picasso speciality.

egg

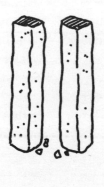

soldiers

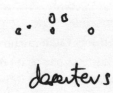

deserters

starfish

tributefish

Squatter's rights | Privacy, a lack of nettles and some large soft leaves.

Stag beetle | Beetle drunk, naked and chained to a lamppost.

Stamp | One place where you will still find a flattering image of a member of the royal family.

Staple, dietary | Drastic attempt to reduce stomach size.

Starting block | Result of athlete failing drugs test.

State-of-the-art | Curious phrase never used about anything remotely artistic but reserved for describing dull bits of technology.

Statesman, elder | Politician who has outlived their earlier poor reputation.

Stations of the Cross | King's and Charing.

Statistic | An ill, dead, or injured person.

Statistics | The triumph of mathematics over political debate.

Stethoscope | Device used by GPs when they choose to actually listen to their patients.

Stitch in time… | Saves running the marathon dressed as a womble.

Stools, between two | Where it is hoped the foot will fall on heavily dog-fouled pavements.

Stream of consciousness | See River of Babble-on.

Stretch of the imagination | A jail sentence served in full.

Subconscious | What whales and dolphins have to be.

Succeed, if at first you don't … | You'll end up owing the banks a fortune.

Suffocated | Died in Suffolk.

Summing up | Period at end of court case when lawyers total up their bills.

Sunday | Formerly a day of rest, now a DIY of rest.

Supermarket | A small hypermarket.

Surface tension | Result of face lift.

Surgical bombing | Military euphemism for bombing likely to result in victims requiring surgery.

past

present

the swearbox: Past & Present

tail wind

T | 1. Tonic. 2. Tax.

Tablespoon | Family-sized helping of cocaine.

Table-talk | Frustrating *Antiques Roadshow* chat prior to the expert's revelation of an item's likely worth.

Tabloid | Newspaper size recognising the trend towards the much smaller modern bathroom.

Taboo, the last | Any taboo prior to the next to be broken is described as the last.

Tacit support | Support always claimed by those without support. See 'Liberal Democrats'.

Tadpole | Ageist term for a pre-adult frog.

Tagging | Criminal act of putting one's name on a train carriage. Past offenders include Connex, WAGN and Silverlink.

Tailback | The happy result of banning docking.

Tails, slugs and snails and puppy dogs' | Contents labelling now required by law on every male human juvenile.

Take it to heart | What the bloodstream does with cholesterol.

Take off | Brief period in which even economy-class passengers get to have reclining seats.

Taken to task | See commuting.

Taking stock | The first stage in recovery from hunger strike.

Talk of the town | What rich people do in the country at weekends.

Talk is cheap | Assertion refuted by lawyers and mobile telephone companies.

Talking shop | Mobile phone outlet.

Talks about talks | The positive outcome of talks about talks about talks.

Tall order | Large latté.

Tamper-proof seal | Amphibious mammal safe from perverts.

Tandem | A welcome attempt to halve the number of noisy, polluting bicycles to be found on roads today.

Tank Engine, Thomas the | Hilarious satire on the privatised railway business in which the Controller gets Fat while the outdated rolling stock and engines suffer breakdowns, accidents and competition from buses. Meanwhile the Islanders' needs are a second-place concern.

Tantric sex | Extended form of lovemaking, and source of the phrase, 'Fancy a longie?'

Tap, phone | An example of democracy in action, i.e. the government listening to the people.

Tapestry, Bayeux | Early form of war-reporting in which the journalists were embroidered rather than embedded.

Tar and feathers | Result of over-microwaving poultry.

Tarmac | Highway surfacing material whose invention seems to have escaped the notice of the majority of purchasers of off-road vehicles.

Tartrazine | Food additive linked to hyperactivity in children and food companies' PR departments.

Tarzan | Aristocrat's son who experiences the most severe example of being sent away to boarding school.

Taste, bad | The jokes about atrocities rather than those atrocities themselves, oddly.

Taste, good | One's own taste reflected in others.

Tasteless | 1. Food with too little ketchup. 2. Film with too much ketchup.

Tax collector | One of the few collectors who prefers not to talk at length in public about their hobby.

Tax, liable to | Euphemism for 'alive'.

Taxidermy | The last chance Britain has of preserving its wildlife.

Tea break | Period in which coffee is consumed.

Teaching assistant | Paracetamol.

Teasel | Sexually provocative weasel.

Tectonics | The study of large cold plates moving very

slowly over the surface of the planet – a factor in both the development of earthquakes and the failure of Little Chef.

Temptation, lead us not into | Lord's Prayer equivalent of Sat Nav.

Ten Commandments | First serious attempt to control criminal behaviour through the use of tablets. Proven highly effective in the area of ass-coveting.

Tentacle | A small tent.

Terminal velocity | The maximum speed with which they can plan and build new airports.

Terrestrial television | Gardening programmes.

Territorial waters | Vichy, Caledonian Spring, Buxton, etc.

Terrorism | The old name for what is now called asymmetrical warfare – presumably because its soldiers are irregular.

Test case | Legal term. A vital procedure for barristers before buying claret.

Test-tube baby | Child born under the sign of Pyrex.

Thankless task | Any task performed by people who have to wear caps and aprons.

Them and us | Misspelled statement of difference. See Them and US.

Theme music | The fifteen-second warning before *EastEnders* properly starts.

Thermocouple | Red-hot lovers.

Thermos | The god of train-spotters.

Thick and thin | How most pop stars prefer their girlfriends.

Thief in the night | About the only professional who still does house calls after 6.

Think tank | Good advice for the first-time driver in Baghdad.

Thirteen | Unlucky for: 1. Some. 2. Parents with children of this age.

Thoughtful | Person who not only buys flowers, but doesn't buy petrol at the same time.

Threatening letters | MRSA, ASBO, OHMS, GBH, HIV, etc.

Three Rs, The | *The Pirates of the Caribbean* trilogy.

Thrillseeker | Person who eats anything without first checking the use-by date.

Throne | Unusual instance of a seat which an older person is expected to give up to a younger one.

Throne, the power behind the | The British tourism and souvenir industries.

Throwaway remark | Observation no longer made to litter louts due to fear of violent response.

Tick, sheep | Mark made by farmer on EU Lamb Subsidy Form.

Tick? what makes him | Alarming question to ask in a Tel Aviv square.

Ticket, dream | An advance supersaver railfare that's available whenever you need it. Plus it's facing the engine. Oh, and on the day, no one sits in any of the seats neighbouring yours.

Tie-in book | Hazard of reading novel on train in to work.

Tie me kangaroo down, sport | Seminal Rolf Harris number abhorred by animal rightists for continuing to associate animal cruelty with 'sport'.

Tight security | 1. Any level of security yet to be exposed as a sham is described as tight. 2. Drunken building guards.

Time, doing | How Stephen Hawking describes his work at parties.

Time-honoured | Cliché used of any pointless ritual with nothing to commend it other than for how long it has been performed.

Time lapse photography | Seemingly the only way of speeding up most roadworks.

Timid | Word used to describe any wild creature which refuses to make an idiot of itself in return for scraps of stale bread.

Timetable, railway | A triumph of hope over experience.

Tinned | Word meaning 'not frozen'.

Tip | A payment made in return for: 1. Good service; 2. Avoiding a scene; 3. Getting council workers to do what they're paid for.

Tissue of lies | See Government White Paper.

TOG | Warmth rating for bed covers. The average cat is about 3, a Chihuahua about 1.5, and a Newfoundland nearly 17.

Toilet-training | Teaching your kids not to use public toilets, especially those on trains.

Toilet-water | The nature of the sea close by many a British resort.

Tomato | A ketchup flavour.

Tonight | Misspelling of 'tonite'.

Toothbrush | Device for promoting tooth-loss through accelerated gum erosion.

Tooth fairies | Sweet little sprites that spirit away children's teeth. Their names are Dee, Kay, and Ginger Vitis.

Top secret | Legend stamped on government documents to ensure their speedy return from phone-boxes, cafes, bus shelters, etc.

Torso | The largest section of the human body that will fit comfortably into a bin liner.

Tortoise | Reptilian victim of excess packaging.

Toss, winning the | A British sporting victory.

Touchtone | Phone allowing customers to play pretty tunes as they dial wrong numbers.

Tourist | 1. A despised foreign visitor. 2. A despised English cricketer.

Towel, Roller | Washroom 'Test-Your-Strength' machine.

Toxic, non- | Safety claim made, intriguingly, for pencil crayons rather than foodstuffs.

Tractor, Chelsea | 1. Nickname for any 4x4 that never leaves SW6. 2. Wiltshire farmer on way to make protest in Whitehall.

Trading estate | Estate with high numbers of drug dealers, stolen car salesmen, unlicensed firearm procurers, etc.

Traditional | Term used to describe any extinct folk practice recently revived to aid the sale of brown bread, beer, or country cottage holidays.

Traffic island | Britain.

Train-spotting | Pointillist approach to railway graffiti.

Transistor radio | Radio so small and, hence, so portable, that it can annoy people anywhere in the world.

Transmission | The spread of: 1. Diseases; 2. Television programmes.

Trappist | About the only religious extremist you won't hear on a radio phone-in.

Tray | Device for carrying large quantities of lager outside the human body.

Tree of knowledge | Gingko, according to health food shops.

Trepanning | Esoteric remedy which most people need like a hole in the head.

Trespass | No doubt by sheer coincidence, a perfect rhyme of 'Press Pass'.

Trial and error | See Retrial.

Trial run | The on-foo escape of prisoners from custody.

Triangle, Bermuda | Area notorious for the eery disappearance of whole aircraft, not just their passengers' luggage.

Trick or treat | Moonlight robbery.

Trolleyed, totally | 1. Drunk.
2. Hospital over-full.

Truant | One of the few traditional games schoolchildren still play.

Trump | In Britain, a vulgar flatus. In the States, a vulgar tycoon.

Truth, the | A legal impediment.

Tsar | Popular epithet given to any public official handed the task of sorting out some pressing social problem, and usually highly accurate in reflecting the same eventual degree of success as that achieved by the last actual Tsar.

Tunes, the Devil has all the best | That's because the Devil gets all the worst colds and sore throats.

Turkish delight | Any Greek set back.

Turkish delight | Any Greek set back.

Turn on, tune in, drop out | 1960s bead-time radicals' rubric.

Turn on, tune in, drop off | Over-60s bedtime radio ritual.

Twenty-four seven | How often one now encounters this Americanism.

Twin town | Siamese tourist attraction.

Two up, two down | Numerical based description of: 1. A modest house; 2. A pre-op transsexual.

Two's company ... | There's an unauthorised gathering. (Old North Korean proverb)

Tzigane | Hungarian gypsy popular with Scrabble fans.

U.F.O.

U | Film and DVD classification. It stands for universal, though many adults and violence-hungry older kids alike seem to think it means unwatchable.

Ubiquitous | 1. Ant and Dec. 2. MRSA. (The latter may prove easier to eradicate.)

UFO | An unidentifiable light in the sky. For city-dwellers this will include most of the constellations, the planets, and in the worst cases of light pollution, even the moon.

Ugly duckling | Duckling contemplating cosmetic surgery, but concerned it will still end up with a really big bill.

Ultrasonic | Level of sound audible only to dogs and those who love complaining to hotel managers.

Unibilical cords | Stretch-fabric trousers worn by expectant mothers.

Umbilical cord | Mother Nature's very own child safety rein.

Umbrage | Spiritual home of disaffected Archers fans.

Umbrella organisation | The Whitehall civil service.

Umpire, tennis | An official so unpopular that he is placed on a high chair out of reach of enraged players.

Umpteen | A teen with the ump. This is pretty much all of them, hence the word's association with a large number.

Unacceptable, wholly | Acceptable, eventually.

Unapproachable | Ex-wife with restraining order.

Unarmed | Pupil at school with metal detectors installed.

Unattended luggage | Another case for the bomb squad.

Unawares, caught | Most venereal diseases.

Unborn child | Child who so far has only been able to hear TV adverts.

Uncalled for | About 10 per cent of all completed dry cleaning.

Uncharitable act | Any act that refuses to appear for free on Comic Relief night.

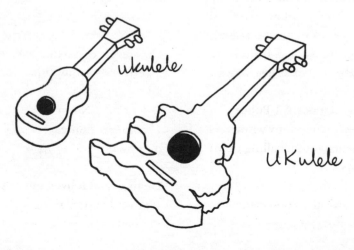

Uncle Tom's Cabin | Now expanded as 'Uncle Tom's Stay-A-While Cabin Complex' and 'Cotton PickersTM Soul-Food Restaurant'.

Unclean! Unclean! | A traditional British beach cry.

Uncommonly good | Modern tautology. Anything good nowadays is, by definition, uncommon.

Uncontrollable urges | Those urges which the sufferer chooses not to control.

Unconventional | Word used to make polite allowance for the behaviour of any person who is bonkers but rich or influential. Everyone else is just a loony.

Uncooperative | Police assessment of any witness with a penchant for falling down stairs.

Uncritical | Food critic when very hungry.

Uncut version | How pretentious, 'auteur theory' bakers like to refer to their yet-to-be-sliced loaves.

Underacting | A base accusation to level at Keith Allen.

Underage drinker | Child at serious risk of damaging their health with cola, aspartame, artificial sweeteners, etc.

Undercoat | The innermost coat worn by any old lady in August.

Underdeveloped | Any large breasts not yet maximally employed in selling lads' mags.

Undergrad | Now reverted to its former name of St Underberg.

Underground movement | A violent sideways jerking with long pauses in between.

undertakers' towels

Underpass | Eloquent proof that the only real thing for which a road will actually be diverted at great expense is another road.

Underprivileged | Self-opinion of privileged people with even more privileged friends.

Understanding | Diplomatic euphemism for the point at which two opposing sides in an argument give up negotiating. They both understand that the other side is wrong.

Understudy | To risk getting a B in one's A levels.

Undertaking, massive | The late Pavarotti's funeral.

Undiscovered | Travel brochure euphemism for that area of the globe that the trade has decided to ruin next.

Unemployment benefit | No longer having to commute.

Unerring | French for an unsmoked kipper.

Unexpected pleasure | Any pleasure afforded by daytime TV.

Unforeseen circumstances | Poor reason for cancelling evening of clairvoyance.

Unguarded moment | Any royal loo-break, presumably.

University challenge | Getting Britons to study science subjects.

University of life | Academic institution with deplorably low entrance requirements.

Unkempt | British film featuring neither Martin nor Gary Kemp.

Unnecessary suffering | See Eurovision song contest.

Unorthodox | Every new detective in every new TV crime series. One who followed procedure precisely would probably prove a refreshing change.

Unparliamentary language | Swearing, rather than the telling of bare-faced lies.

Unpopular | Synonym for: 1. French; 2. Healthy; 3. British; rather than American; 4. Sensible; 5. Educational.

Unprincipled | Elected.

Unprintable | See Lawyer.

Unprofessional conduct | Working for free.

Unqualified success | TV funster Paul Merton.

Unquiet grave | Corpse buried with mobile phone.

Unrest | TV news cliché. The throwing of stones in foreign town centres.

Unscripted | Any simple question which puts a politician off his stride.

Unspeakable acts | Mime artists.

Unspoilt countryside | Obviously poor building land.

Unstoppable | Bus with driver over-running end of shift.

Unswerving loyalty | Loyalty yet to be made a better offer.

Unwashed, the great | Organic vegetables.

Upright citizen | Still-sober citizen.

Useful life | What many civil servants could yet be capable of leading.

User-friendly | Odd term implying that some new machines are not actually designed with purchasers in mind.

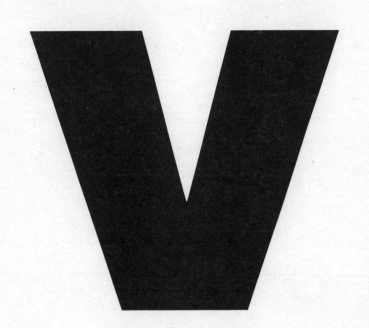

V | Sociable letter responsible for bringing so many people together: Regina v Smith, Smith v Smith, England v Scotland, etc.

Vaccination programme | Yet another MMR documentary.

Vague recollection | Perfect recollection obscured merely by the fear of blame.

Valentine's day | Occasion each year when men send their loved ones flowers – and sometimes their wives get them too.

Valuation | Process by which rival estate agents attempt to estimate just how much your house sale would mean to them.

Valve, safety | Term used to dignify any anti-social act which distracts people from carrying out some even worse anti-social act. Attempting to make them behave better is said to be a 'pressure cooker'.

Vandal | One who wilfully damages property or land without a contract from the government.

Vanilla | Exotic ice-cream-flavoured spice.

Vanishing point | That point immediately after handing over a large amount of money to a cowboy company when they suddenly disappear for ever from their premises.

Veal | Meat from cows denied the chance to grow up and develop BSE.

Vegetarian | The one person at a barbecue with pleasant-tasting unburnt, edible food.

Velveteen | A difficult age for velvet.

Veneer | Coating applied to valuable chipboard to protect it from harm.

Venerable | Polite euphemism for 'successful but past it'.

Venture, this exciting new | The past tense of 'this spectacular business failure'.

Vermin | Category into which nearly all the most popular cartoon animals fall.

Verse, free | Use of the word 'free' as a synonym for 'rubbish'. See also free jazz, free gift, free flight offer, etc.

Vertigo | Classic Hitchcock film inspiring much zany DVD shop humour, e.g. Customer: 'Do you have *Vertigo*?' Assistant: 'No, I live above the premises!'

Veto | The least co-operative of the Sackville-Wests.

Vexed | What German Barbour jackets are.

Via | The cockneys' favourite Sackville-West.

Vicar | 1. A Church of England minister. 2. A character often encountered in farce (see 1).

Vice Squad | A humorously named Soho joinery firm.

Victim support | See Crutches.

Victoria cross | Becks on more magazine covers than her.

Victorian values | 1. An outmoded belief in God, the family, side-whiskers, child labour, and cholera. 2. Now appreciated only by those in the antiques trade.

Village | Hampstead's greatest deception. In London the term means essentially any small area whose street name-plates still differ from the standard council issue. To estate agents it may consist of no more than a single street with an all-night store at one end.

Village idiot | An indigenous yokel who sells the family cottage too cheaply too soon.

Vintage | Euphemism for 'rubbish, but old rubbish', and used as a poor excuse for re-running bad films and sitcoms on TV, e.g. 'Vintage comedy now on BBC1 as the staff of Grace Brothers ask 'Are You Being ...?' etc.

VIP lounge | Place where dull celebrities and businessmen pay more to pass the same amount of time waiting in the same airport for the same plane as poor people.

Virgin olive oil, extra | The olive oil of choice for martyrs.

Virtue | Gesundheit.

Vital signs | £, €, $, etc.

Vital statistics | Football results.

Viviparous | Bringing forth young alive, rather than laying eggs like Baroness Thatcher.

Vocation | Defined as any badly paid job which someone has taken out of choice.

Vocational guidance | Advising your friends not to become teachers or nurses.

Voicemail | Due to a high level of interest we are currently unable to bring you this definition. Please close the book and try again later.

Volatile situation | A peaceful situation plus television cameras.

Vol-au-vent | Rare French winged vole.

Voluntary contributions | Contributions which one has to be asked to make.

Vomit | An anagram of 'Vimto'.

Vote | Handy source of Zimbabwean scrap paper.

Vowels | In Loyd Grossman's alphabet, those letter with stretchmarks.

V-sign | The sign of the cross.

Vulgar fraction | 4Q/2.

walrus moustache

Wafer | Common appeal for delay as in 'Wafer me! I can't walk that fast...' etc.

Wage-slave | Japanese term of endearment.

Waggish | Funny.

WAG-ish | Hilarious.

Waistline | The 24-hour confidential telephone counselling service for problem eaters.

Wake the dead, enough to | A large amount of: 1. Noise; 2. Amphetamines.

Wake up England! | Former 1930s anti-Nazi rallying cry. Now what car alarms do every night.

Wales, Prince of | Title naturally given to that royal who owns most of Cornwall.

Walk-on role | What carpeting has in the homes of actors.

Walking stick | Catwalk fashion model.

Walks of life, people from different | A *Monty Python* sketch.

Walrus | About the only large grey thing that looks better with a moustache.

Wanted by the police | More police, long-handled batons, stop and search, basically anything that makes them look more American.

War crimes | Crimes committed by those who have lost a war.

Warder | What American health bores choose instead of alcohol.

Warehouse | A large storage space in which, well, we might have another one, but, you know, it could be two or three weeks until our next delivery. Have you tried our Watford branch?

Warm front | Result of high pressure – especially in overcrowded trains.

Warm personality | Character trait noticed in ugly people.

Warmer! You're getting | Children's thimble-hunting

cry, now taken up by global ecologists.

Warning, flood | The gist of every right-wing MP's speech on unimigration.

Warning, a few words of | 'New', 'Improved', 'Advanced', 'Tastier than ever', 'Alcohol-free', etc.

Warped mind | MiND.

Warranty, one year | Statutory guarantee that by law must accompany any product with a working lifespan of exactly 366 days.

Wartime | From 0000 to 2400 hours, daily.

Wash and go | 1. An overhyped shampoo. 2. The landowner's plea to New Age travellers.

Wash your hands, now | 1. Sign always found in toilets next to a filthy roller towel. 2. US foreign policy.

Wasp | An oddity of nature – a creature with a tiny waist, yet it spends all its time in cake shops.

Wastage, natural | Extinction.

Waste of breath | 1. Karaoke. 2. The harmonica.

Waste paper | 1. Labour election leaflets in the south of England. 2. Tory election leaflets in Scotland. 3. All Green Party leaflets, ironically.

Wasting police time | Protesting your innocence if young, black or Muslim.

Watchword | Quartz.

Watered down | Distressing result of the combination of a weak bladder and a duvet.

Waterlogged | Result of domestic meter being fitted.

Watershed | TV term for 9pm. That time after which children must go to their rooms in order to keep watching the television.

Waves, it comes in | Used toilet paper, rotting seaweed, disposable nappies, old condoms, tampons, etc.

Weakness, fundamental | Piles.

Wealth creation | See Forgery.

Wear down | What geese do.

Weasel-word | Pop.

Weather | British synonym for rain, as in 'Just look at the weather …'

Weather balloon | How one fondly hopes the Establishment on other planets explains our satellites to its people.

Weather-beaten | What most British summer sporting fixtures are.

Weather forecast, long range | Any wildly inaccurate weather prediction made from the safety of a distant TV studio.

Weather pitch, all- | The TV meteorologists' spiel.

Weatherman, TV | A man who talks too quickly while pointing to a rapidly changing set of baffling electronic images – which we know he can't actually see – and then expects us to take him seriously. His career goal is to be impersonated by a comedian.

Weather, under the Some irritating little note saying 'Sponsored by Powergen' etc.

Wedding ring | See Wife-swapping circle.

Wedlock | Type of lock easily undone nowadays.

Weed, the dreaded | According

to age, either stinging nettles, dope or tobacco.

Week | Name given to any marketing exercise which lasts for up to seven days, e.g. 'National Sausage Week'.

Weekend break | Sunday soccer league sporting injury.

Weight machine, I speak your | Machine known only to cartoonists.

Weekend, dirty | DIY on Saturday, gardening on Sunday.

Weighty matters | Those individually trivial matters which go to make up each back-breaking edition of the *Sunday Times*.

Welcome to Wales | What most people would say the Welsh people are.

Well as can be expected, as | Ill

time.

Well disposed | Recycled.

Well trained | What the subsequent accident inquiry showed that Jack and Jill patently were not. They were ordered to attend a compulsory Bucket Management course.

Wheelie-bin | Rodent meals on wheels.

Where angels fear to tread | Area with high dog ownership.

Wench | Any female film extra in a bodice.

Wendy house | Play home now banned from schools for giving children an unrealistic expectation of future home ownership.

When push comes to shove | Rush hour on the Tube.

Where do you get your ideas? | Tedious question which only writers and the insane get asked. The insane attempt to answer it.

Werewolf | Member of a dangerous sect: the Full-Moonies.

Westernise | Round, not slitty, as Prince Philip would rush to explain.

Whispering campaign | Doomed attempt by train companies to promote considerate use of mobiles.

Wet blanket | Forgotten patient in care home.

Whispering grass | Grass trying hard not to be overheard by Prince Charles.

Wheelbarrow | Novelty wallet given to city bankers at bonus

Whistler's Mother | Popular title for the Victorian painting more accurately known as *That*

Miserable Old Bat In The Chair.

Whizz kid | Child on high dose of Ritalin.

Whole food | Eating four quarter-pounders at once.

W.I. | A brazen band of blue-rinsed brigands who laugh in the face of the law with their EU-proscribed scone and jam-making activities.

Wicked stepmother | Youth-speak for a superlative stepmother, as in 'Hey, man!

You gotta wicked stepmother!'

Wicket, slow | Wicket with the intelligence of the average England selector.

Wideboy | 1. Man with criminal habits. 2. Child with criminal diet.

Widening scheme, road | Euphemism for what is more alarmingly a countryside narrowing scheme.

Wilderness, voice in the | 'Get orf moi land!'

weeping

on-prozac

willows

Wildflowers | Those plants that have to be dug up surreptitiously from woods rather than shoplifted from garden centres.

Wildfowl Trust | What duck-hunters gain before blasting their quarry from the water.

Wildlife | Name given by townies to creatures killed by farmers.

Wind blows, when the | Faults in double-glazing become apparent.

Windbreak | A few days respite from the Atkins diet.

Window of opportunity | Burglar's slang for an open window.

Windswept | How the streets are kept clean in Britain's poorer boroughs.

Wine, British | Blended foreign wine for which this gallant nation nobly takes the blame.

Winged horse | Horse grazed by pellet fired by vandal with air rifle.

Winker Watson | Famous

Winning post | Begging letters following Lottery jackpot.

Dandy comic schoolboy lucky never to have encountered the Reverend Spooner.
Winning that counts, it's not the ... | It's the fee for taking part. (Old English proverb.)

Wisdom of the ancients | Only possible explanation for how primitive men could site Stonehenge so that some 3000 years later it could be within walking distance of the main road.

Wisdom teeth | On average, the last teeth that Britons have filled.

Wish upon a star, when you | 1. It turns out to be some fool man-made satellite. 2. You end up getting eaten by a whale.

Wit | Defined by TV as jokes made by people sitting down.

Witchcraft | A broomstick.

Wive's tale, old | Evidence given in divorce court.

Woad | How Britons got blue in the face before roadrage.

Wobbly, throw a | 1. To become suddenly angry. 2. Sumo-wrestling in a nutshell.

Womaniser | Oestrogen.

Women's issues | *Hello!, Bella!, Top Sante, OK!,* etc.

Woollen underwear | See Seven year itch.

Wood engravings | AK 4 JS, SKINS RULE, FUK, WANKAS, etc.

Word of mouth | Gobsmacked.

Word on the streets, the | No entry, Bus lane, Look right, etc.

Workmanlike | 1. Late. 2. Slow.

Work hard, play hard | Vinnie Jones's acting technique.

Working from home | See Telivised Test Cricket.

Work, whistle while you | What faulty hearing aids do.

Work-to-rule | Prince Charles's *modus operandi*.

World | Term meaning: 1. 'Foreign' or 'non-commercial', as in world cinema, world music, world peace, etc; 2. 'North American' or 'highly commercial', as in

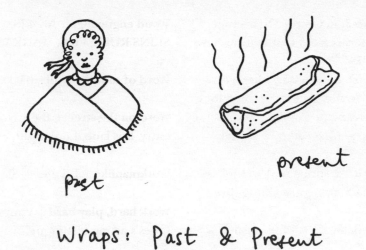

past

present

Wraps: Past & Present

World Series, World Wrestling Federation, Disney World, etc.

Worst-case scenario | That your luggage will be the cheapest, most battered and most damaged item on the airport carousel.

Wrinkle | A face rift.

Wrist-watch | Watch kept by potential thief on Rolex Oyster wearer.

Writing on the wall | 'Please do not write on this wall'.

X | 1. The newspaper sign of the cross, as in 'What the XXXX is going on?' etc.
2. Roman numeral used to conceal the age of TV repeats.
3. An old film classification certificate, now roughly equivilent to today's 'PG'.
4. A kiss.

XX | Two kisses.

XXX | Porn.

XXXX | Lager.

XXXXX | Pools coupon.

XXXXXL | Average American clothing size

X Factor | Legend on ancient Roman sun tan oils.

Xmas | Popular festival, made to sound like a skin condition.

Xenophobia | The Englishman's hatred of foreigners – from the Latin words 'xenos' and 'phobos'.

X-rays | 1. How Salman Rushdie still reads his post.
2. What 'Super-waif' modelling shoots are often mistaken for.

X-ray Specs | The first time many males realise that technology won't necessarily bring them happiness. It is also the first time many males choose to ignore the fact and continue to live in hope.

XS | The level to which tacky abbreviations are used nowadays.

Xylophone | Tuned kindling.

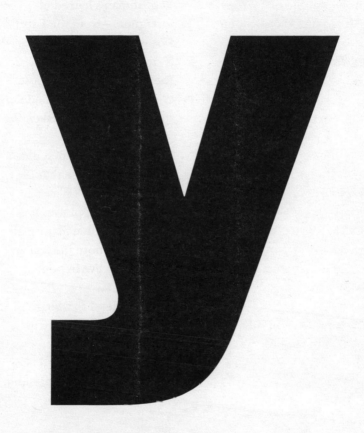

yaardvark (NB: exactly 3 ~~feet~~)

Y | Acronym for 'young' as in YM – Young Men, YW – Young Women, and YI – Young Geordies.

Yahoo | 1. Internet search engine. 2. Cry of delight at actually finding something relevant on the internet.

Yamaha | A type of loud motorbike or electronic organ. From the Japanese for 'irritating noise'.

Yard | A measure greater than the metre in every respect but length.

Yard of ale | See Beer garden.

Yardstick | A measure of quality, and therefore naturally associated with far-off pre-decimal days.

Y chromosome | The one with the gene for peeing standing up.

Year in, year out | Recidivist's prison schedule.

Yellow belly | Result of incorrect use of instant tan cream.

Yellow peril | 1. Wheel-clamp. 2. Egg yolk.

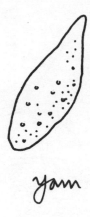

yam

yamnot

Yes and no | Two of the shorter, less favoured answers available to politicians for use in interviews.

Yoghurt | See Yogourt.

Yogourt | See Yogurt.

Yogurt | Fast becoming the only culture devoured in the average home. See also 'Yoghurt' and 'Yogourt'.

Y-fronts | Popular British underpants which apparently took 25 prototypes to perfect, the A-fronts and K-fronts being particularly perplexing, and the O-fronts totally impractical.

Yugoslavia | The former name for what is now known as 'the Former Yugoslavia'.

Yule log | Complex tax and VAT records kept by Father Christmas.

Z

Z | Low-scoring letter in most Eastern European Scrabble sets.

Zebra | A bar-coded horse.

Zero tolerance | The strange ability of Tynesiders to not notice the cold.

Zimmer | Old person's frame of reference.

Zinc | What Poirot does with ees leetle grey zells.

Zodiac | The first 12 signs of madness.

Zoetrope | Device producing an illusion of movement. See also M25.

Zymology | The study of fermentation. It comes at the very end of most English dictionaries, because by this point both author and audience could do with a drink.

Zzzzzz | 1. Onomatopoeic representation of the buzz in the House of Lords. 2. Author after finally finishing *This Septic Isle.*

traditional
snowman

zero carbon
snowman